The Making of a Disciple

The Making of a Disciple

Character Studies in the Gospel of John

EDWARD W. WATSON
MARTIN M. CULY

CASCADE *Books* · Eugene, Oregon

THE MAKING OF A DISCIPLE
Character Studies in the Gospel of John

Copyright © 2021 Edward W. Watson and Martin M. Culy. All rights reserved. Except for brief quotations in critical publications or reviews, no part of this book may be reproduced in any manner without prior written permission from the publisher. Write: Permissions, Wipf and Stock Publishers, 199 W. 8th Ave., Suite 3, Eugene, OR 97401.

Cascade Books
An Imprint of Wipf and Stock Publishers
199 W. 8th Ave., Suite 3
Eugene, OR 97401

www.wipfandstock.com

PAPERBACK ISBN: 978-1-7252-9876-7
HARDCOVER ISBN: 978-1-7252-9877-4
EBOOK ISBN: 978-1-7252-9878-1

Cataloguing-in-Publication data:

Names: Watson, Edward W., author. | Culy, Martin M., author.

Title: The making of a disciple : character studies in the Gospel of John / by Edward W. Watson and Martin M. Culy.

Description: Eugene, OR: Cascade Books, 2021 | Includes bibliographical references and index.

Identifiers: ISBN 978-1-7252-9876-7 (paperback) | ISBN 978-1-7252-9877-4 (hardcover) | ISBN 978-1-7252-9878-1 (ebook)

Subjects: LCSH: Bible. John—Criticism, interpretation, etc. | Jesus Christ—Friends and associates | Characters and characteristics in the Bible.

Classification: BS2615.52 M35 2021 (print) | BS2615.52 (ebook)

Scripture quotations marked (NRSV) are from the New Revised Standard Version Bible, copyright © 1989 National Council of the Churches of Christ in the United States of America. Used by permission. All rights reserved worldwide.

Scripture quotations marked (NIV) are taken from the Holy Bible, New International Version®, NIV®. Copyright © 1973, 1978, 1984, 2011 by Biblica, Inc.™ Used by permission of Zondervan. All rights reserved worldwide. www.zondervan.com The "NIV" and "New International Version" are trademarks registered in the United

States Patent and Trademark Office by Biblica, Inc.™

Scripture quotations marked (ESV) are taken from The Holy Bible, English Standard Version®, copyright © 2001 by Crossway, a publishing ministry of Good News Publishers. Used by permission. All rights reserved.

Scripture quotations marked (NET) are taken from the NET Bible® copyright ©1996-2017 by Biblical Studies Press, L.L.C. Used by permission. http://netbible.com. All rights reserved.

Scripture quotations marked (CSB) are taken from the Christian Standard Bible® Copyright© 2017 by Holman Bible Publishers. Christian Standard Bible® and CSB® are federally registered trademarks of Holman Bible Publishers. Used by permission.

Contents

Preface ix

1: Setting the Stage 1

2: John the Baptist, Andrew, and Philip:
Pointing Others to Jesus 17

3: Nicodemus: A Confusing Encounter with Jesus 26

4: The Samaritan Woman:
A Transformational Encounter with Jesus 39

5: The Healing of the Royal Official's Son:
A Faith-Building Encounter with Jesus 53

6: The Healing of the Sick Man at the Pool:
A Selfish Encounter with Jesus 61

7: The Healing of the Blind Man:
A Life-Changing Encounter with Jesus 70

8: Mary and Martha, Mary and Judas:
Faith, Devotion, and Fake Discipleship 84

9: Peter and the Beloved Disciple:
Passionate Devotion, Steady Devotion 94

Contents

10: Thomas: More than a Doubter 112

11: The Gospel of John and Future Disciples 120

Bibliography 127
Author Index 131

Preface

THE GOSPEL OF JOHN holds a special place in our hearts. Martin wrote and later published his doctoral dissertation on the Gospel of John[1] and has recently produced curriculum to help others teach this important book of the Bible. Edward wrote a thesis on the Gospel of John and later contributed a chapter on John's Gospel to a monograph[2] and served as the translator of the Gospel of John for the *New Tyndale Version*. The Gospel of John was the first book of the Bible that Martin read after becoming a follower of Jesus and the first book that he taught to others. Edward has taught the Gospel of John for many years at both the undergraduate and graduate levels and we have both preached and taught this book in the church. What follows, then, is the result of decades of reflection on the Gospel of John, reflections that have left us both fascinated, in particular, with how this book of the Bible presents us with intriguing characters who push us to consider our own responses to Jesus and his teachings.

The scholarly literature on characters and characterization in the Gospel of John has grown considerably in recent years. The focus, however, has typically been more on scholarly analysis than on how such studies should impact the life of disciples today. In our view, the task of exegesis is never complete until we have grappled with the "So what?" questions that the text presents to us. And that will be our focus in what follows. We will examine how major characters in the Gospel of John are used to shape our understanding of what an authentic, growing disciple of Jesus should look like.

For those who are interested in exploring further the scholarly works that have informed what follows, we would recommend especially the foundational works of Alter, Berlin, Marguerat and Bourquin, and Culpepper, as well as the more recent important works of Bennema, Skinner, and Hunt,

1. Culy, *Echoes*.
2. Watson and Watson, "Love of God," 153–70.

Preface

Tolmie, and Zimmermann.[3] We have also interacted with many of the more helpful commentaries on the Gospel of John. Our hope and prayer is that as we take a fresh look at the characters who encounter Jesus in the Gospel of John, readers will see more clearly not only who Jesus is and what he has done, but also the life that he calls every genuine disciple to embrace. As the apostle John himself notes, the stakes are high. Life and death are on the line: "But these are written so that you may come to believe that Jesus is the Messiah, the Son of God, and that through believing you may have life in his name" (20:31).[4] And for those who have life in his name, there is still the question of whether or not that life will be the abundant life that Jesus promises to those who truly embrace the path of discipleship (10:10).

---

3. Alter, *The Art of Biblical Narrative*; Berlin, *Poetics*; Marguerat and Bourquin, *How to Read Bible Stories*; Culpepper, *Anatomy*; Bennema, *Encountering Jesus*; Bennema, "A Theory of Character"; Skinner, *Characters and Characterization*; Hunt, Tolmie, and Zimmermann, *Character Studies*.

4. All Scripture quotations are taken from the NRSV unless otherwise noted.

1

Setting the Stage

THE GOSPEL OF JOHN was written to help readers "get it right about Jesus," and by getting it right to find life through him. To accomplish this goal, the apostle John[1] provides a selection of accounts from the life of Jesus that reveal particular aspects of his identity, mission, and message, in part through his interactions with various characters. As these characters encounter Jesus, they are forced to decide how they will respond to his self-revelation and to his teachings. We will discover that some embrace what Jesus offers and have their lives transformed, while others reject Jesus and his teachings. Like the characters he describes, the apostle John expects his readers to decide how they will respond to the person and message of Jesus. Will they turn to him in faith, receive the life that he offers, and become his disciples, or will they reject him like many in Jesus' day did?

John's choice of which characters to include in his gospel and his account of their responses to Jesus paint a vivid picture of what constitutes both saving faith and genuine discipleship. Quite often, the nature of the discipleship Jesus calls his followers to embrace is made clear through contrasting certain characters. One character is presented alongside another, inviting readers to compare and contrast their responses to Jesus and the spiritual consequences of those responses. The following chapters will examine a number of examples of this literary phenomenon of what we might call "character pairs" and explore how John uses this literary device to urge his readers to respond to Jesus as true disciples and thus experience fullness of joy (15:11).

---

1. We will assume the traditional view that the apostle John wrote the Gospel of John.

The Making of a Disciple

The Gospel of John was, first and foremost, directed at those who had already embraced Jesus as "the Lamb of God who takes away the sin of the world" (1:29). Such followers of Jesus, however, were still faced with a daily choice: Would they "continue in his word" and thus truly be his disciples (8:31)? That, in fact, is the only way to know the truth and be set free by it (8:32). In other words, experiencing the abundant life that Jesus came to give (10:10) requires that Jesus' disciples embrace him on *his* terms, embracing not only what he has done for them through his death and resurrection, but also embracing *all* that he teaches. Many in Jesus' day liked him. Many were even eager to make Jesus their king (6:15). But the more that Jesus taught, the fewer were those who chose to continue following him (6:66), because the more he taught the less he fit their expectations of who he should be. This is why the Gospel of John is so important for those today who want to be or claim to be disciples of Jesus. According to the Gospel of John, a disciple of Jesus is one who continues in Jesus' words or teachings, and the apostle John has provided us with not only extended teachings from Jesus, but also with numerous examples of what it looks like to either embrace his teachings or reject them.

Our goal in what follows, then, will be to study the most important characters in the Gospel of John, giving attention to how they compare and contrast with other characters, in order to determine what the Gospel of John teaches us through these characters about the nature of genuine discipleship. As we will see, faith responses can vary considerably and still be appropriate responses to Jesus. Before we begin, though, we first need to situate our study in the context of other works on discipleship in the Gospel of John, introduce how characters and characterization work within biblical narrative, and address some of the other literary strategies and motifs that John utilizes to teach us about discipleship.

Recent Studies on Discipleship in the Gospel of John

Although the study of discipleship in the Gospel of John has historically been limited compared to the Synoptic Gospels, there have been a number of notable studies in recent decades.[2] Our goal here is not to survey earlier scholarship. Rather, we will mention just two recent studies to illustrate how our work builds on but is distinct from earlier works. Melvyn

---

2. For a helpful overview of studies on discipleship in the Gospel of John from 1970–2000, see Chennattu, *Johannine Discipleship*, 1–22.

R. Hillmer, for example, focuses on verbs of relationship and action in the Gospel of John that relate to discipleship (e.g., "believe," "know," "follow," "abide/remain," and "keep/obey").[3] He rightly concludes that "discipleship as action is directly related to relationship with Jesus."[4] In other words, based on the language of discipleship that is used in the Gospel of John, we can conclude that discipleship involves following Jesus, bearing fruit, obeying Jesus' commands, keeping his words, serving him, and loving one another.[5] Similarly, Edward Klink focuses on the process or stages of discipleship as seen in the concepts of "following," "believing," and "remaining" in Jesus, and he highlights these as critical features of John's rhetorical strategy.[6] Klink rightly maintains that the marks of true discipleship found in the Gospel of John flow out of one's position in God through Christ, one's participation in the service of Christ, one's participation in the life of God, and one's presentation of the love of God.[7]

Both of these works focus on words, themes, and rhetorical structures to identify the nature of authentic discipleship that is presented in the Gospel of John. Our study, on the other hand, will focus on how the narrator of the Gospel of John utilizes accounts of particular characters to showcase possible responses to Jesus. In doing so, he also showcases what it means to respond to Jesus as his disciple. In other words, the apostle John selectively includes particular characters and presents them alongside other characters not simply to describe how Jesus "revealed his glory" (2:11) or taught particular truths, but also to present to readers a range of both appropriate and inappropriate responses to Jesus for them to either emulate or reject.

Characters and Characterization in Biblical Narrative

This approach to the characters in the Gospel of John is in line with how characters are used elsewhere in biblical narratives. Writers included particular characters with specific traits and personalities as tools to develop the plot, advance the story, and reveal the message(s) the writer intended for readers to take away from the story. Narrative critics describe characters in a variety of ways. Some simply divide characters into "flat" and "round"

3. Hillmer, "They Believed in Him," 77–97.
4. Hillmer, "They Believed in Him," 92.
5. Hillmer, "They Believed in Him," 92.
6. Klink, "Come and See," 60–75.
7. Klink, "Come and See," 68–74.

characters. Flat characters do not stand out as individuals. They are not fleshed out or developed in the narrative like round characters are. They help the story to work as a story, but readers do not experience them as people who make decisions, have feelings, etc. Others prefer a threefold division: "full-fledged character," "type," and "agent." Full-fledged characters are fleshed out more fully in the narrative and are thus parallel to "round" characters. Types, on the other hand, are characters that are stereotypical representations of a particular type or class of people. They have a range of traits, but those traits are stereotypical rather than individual and specific. Finally, agents are characters that are merely a part of the plot or setting but are not developed. They have effects on the plot and on other characters, but they are not important as individuals, and nothing of their individual characteristics or feelings is revealed.

Ultimately, the choice of labels is not as important as understanding the distinctions between round or full-fledged characters and other characters. The message of a narrative will, to a great degree, be communicated through the words and actions of full-fledged or round characters and the consequences of their actions. Many of these major characters will be dynamic or multi-dimensional in nature and sometimes surprise the reader by how they change or develop throughout the course of the narrative, whether for better or worse. And as the narrator reveals particular character traits through a character's actions and speech, readers are presented with opportunities to identify with those characters on a personal level and learn from both the character's successes and failures. While this may also take place, to a lesser degree, in what some call "types," we should not expect agents or "flat" characters to be used in such ways.

What does the distinction between major characters ("round" or "full-fledged") and other characters ("flat" or "agents") look like in practice? If we consider the character of Bathsheba in 2 Sam 11, for example, we find that she is a flat character or merely an agent. She is presented as a beautiful woman and the object of David's lust, who is identified primarily in terms of her relationship to her father and husband (2 Sam 11:3). We are then told that David sent for her, slept with her, and she returned home. Even when we learn of her crisis pregnancy, we are simply told: "*The woman* conceived and she sent and told David, 'I am pregnant'" (2 Sam 11:5), with no focus on her as an individual with feelings and concerns in this crisis situation. And after David murdered her husband, the narrative simply concludes: "When the wife of Uriah heard that her husband was dead, she made lamentation for him. When the mourning was over, David sent and brought her to his house, and she became his wife, and bore him a son. But the thing that David had done displeased the Lord" (2 Sam 11:26–27). Berlin sums up the conclusion of the narrative this way: "One and a half cold, terse verses to sum up the condition of the woman who has had an adulterous affair [or been legally raped], become pregnant, lost her husband, married her lover, the king of Israel, and borne his child! These are crucial events in the life of any woman, yet we are not told how they affected Bathsheba."[8] Why? Because Bathsheba is not a full-fledged character in this passage. The story is not about Bathsheba; it is about David. So, the meaning of the narrative is not revealed through Bathsheba's character and actions, but rather through David's character and actions. And this is signaled to the reader by the way the narrator chooses to present each of these characters (either "round" or "flat"). Berlin rightly concludes that Bathsheba is "a complete non-person" in this narrative. "She is not even a minor character, but simply part of the plot."[9] Thus, for a modern preacher to claim, for example, that we should learn a lesson about the importance of modesty from Bathsheba's actions in 2 Sam 11 ("Don't bathe where people can see you!") would be completely foreign to the message of this passage. In contrast, when Bathsheba appears in 1 Kings 1, she is a full-fledged character and her actions and their consequences are an integral part of the meaning of that passage.

Not surprisingly, there has been some recent debate regarding how characters in the Gospel of John should be viewed and the degree to which the narrator uses characters to represent appropriate or inappropriate responses to Jesus.[10] There is actually a very long history of viewing most characters in the Gospel of John as mere types of individuals rather than as historical persons,[11] and some scholars view the characters in the Gospel of John purely in terms of their representative capacity.[12] In other words, these scholars believe that John's characters are presented as stereotypes that are typically used to focus on a particular trait and/or illustrate a particular faith response to Jesus.[13] Culpepper, for example, in his influential study, posits that most of the characters presented in the Gospel of John exist for

---

8. Berlin, *Poetics*, 26.
9. Berlin, *Poetics*, 27.
10. See Collins, "Representative Figures," 1–45.
11. Collins, "Representative Figures," 1.
12. Collins, "Representative Figures," 7–8.
13. Collins, "Representative Figures," 8.

the sole purpose of moving the plot forward by appearing "on the literary stage only long enough to fulfill their role in the evangelist's representation of Jesus and the response to him."[14] It is thus "difficult to form an impression of them as 'autonomous beings.'"[15] Indeed, Culpepper suggests that "when any of the minor characters conveys an impression of personhood it is usually the personification of a single trait."[16]

While most characters in the Gospel of John have little character development, we would suggest that some are more dynamic in nature. Indeed, Bennema has challenged the idea that most Johannine characters are flat and that their inclusion in the narrative serves only to highlight Jesus and represent a potential response to him. Bennema argues that many of John's characters are in fact presented as round characters with multiple traits and with the ability to develop and change.[17] With Bennema, we maintain that although the characters in John's Gospel present us with representative responses to Jesus, just as other major characters do throughout biblical narratives, many demonstrate character development and growth in discipleship as a result of their repeated encounters with Jesus. This should not surprise us given the fact that John is describing the response of real, historical individuals and groups to Jesus' teachings and actions.

In what follows, we will see that many characters in the Gospel of John are not only presented as models of how to respond to Jesus (or not respond!), but also as characters whose progressive movement toward faith and devotion to Jesus presents readers with opportunities to move forward in their own discipleship.[18] So, while the characters in the Gospel of John must not be reduced to mere "types," their various reactions to Jesus and his teachings do represent potential human responses to Jesus and the revelation he brings that are intended to provoke particular reactions from the reader.[19]

It is to be expected that the introduction of characters throughout the Gospel of John revolve around the character of Jesus. After all, the Gospel of John is a biography and the narrative flow of biographies revolves around

---

14. Culpepper, *Anatomy*, 102.
15. Culpepper, *Anatomy*, 102.
16. Culpepper, *Anatomy*, 102.
17. Bennema, "Theory of Character," 376–77. For additional comments on flat and round characters, see Culpepper, *Anatomy*, 102.
18. See Bennema, "Theory of Character," 402–9.
19. Bennema, "Comprehensive Approach," 56.

a central character. Thus, the events in Jesus' life that John chooses to include in his gospel function "to draw out various aspects of Jesus' character by supplying personalities and situations with which he can interact, and to illustrate a spectrum of alternative responses to him."[20] Moreover, John uses the speech and actions of certain characters to present the reader with opportunities to evaluate their faith responses to Jesus and identify whether their responses are worthy of imitation or should be rejected. Ultimately, these characters serve to help drive readers to John's purpose in writing his gospel: a response to Jesus that results in eternal life (20:31) and abundant life (10:10).

Discipleship and Character Relatability in Biblical Narrative

At its core, Christian discipleship is simply the process of becoming more like Jesus.[21] In the Gospel of John, though, we immediately face a problem. From the opening words, Jesus is presented as God in the flesh (1:1, 14). How, then, can anyone ever expect to be like him in this life, given our severe human limitations? Perhaps precisely because the Gospel of John focuses so strongly on Jesus' divinity, it also presents us with a range of other characters who represent very relatable human examples of possible responses to Jesus in the nitty-gritty of everyday life. And we discover not only characters who excelled in faith and obedience, but also characters with deep flaws that caused them to fail to follow Jesus. How we choose to identify with these characters will significantly impact our own status and potential growth as disciples.

Bible readers are accustomed to making these sorts of choices as they encounter a wide range of characters throughout the biblical narrative. Most of us are eager to imitate Abraham's example of faith, who when told by God to leave everything that represented the good life in his culture, responded with obedience (Gen 12). On the other hand, we want to avoid following Abraham's example of trying to "help God out" by impregnating

---

20. Moore, *Literary Criticism and the Gospels*, 49.

21. Michael J. Wilkins states: "when we speak of Christian discipleship and discipling we are speaking of what it means to grow as a Christian in every area of life . . . discipleship and discipling imply the process of becoming like Jesus Christ. Discipleship and discipling mean living a fully human life in this world in union with Jesus Christ and growing in conformity to his image." Wilkins, *Following the Master*, 41–42.

Hagar, his wife's servant, rather than waiting on God to fulfill his promise (Gen 16). Similarly, though most of us would like to be used by God like Moses to accomplish great things, we can easily relate to Moses's doubts regarding his own weaknesses and his lack of trust in the Lord at times (Exod 3:11; 4:1, 10). And all us would like to be a person after God's own heart like David (1 Sam 13:14), but we also recognize that we have hearts that are prone to wander like David's (2 Sam 11).

The mixed quality that we find in these and many other Old Testament characters can easily lead disciples of Jesus to despair. That is only the case, though, if they miss the whole point of the new covenant that God has established through the Lamb of God who takes away the sin of the world (John 1:29, 35) and who makes it possible for deeply flawed human beings to become born again (John 3:3) disciples of Jesus who live with new hearts (Ezek 36:26), upon which God has written his laws (Jer 31:33), and who enjoy the presence of the Holy Spirit who empowers them to follow God's commands (Ezek 36:27). And New Testament accounts of character development like we will see in the Gospel of John are there, in part, to reveal what that new covenant promise of transformation looks like in real life.

Key Literary Devices and Motifs in the Gospel of John

Individual portraits of disciples and non-disciples in the Gospel of John, of course, must be read within the context of the Gospel of John as a whole, a narrative that makes use of a wide range of literary devices and distinctive literary motifs to help communicate its message. While we have no intention of exploring John's literary devices broadly, given the focus of this study, familiarizing ourselves with a few of them will help us more effectively analyze John's presentation of characters and the lessons he intends to teach us through them.

Comparison and Contrast

Biblical narratives often develop characters by presenting those characters alongside other characters and inviting readers to notice how they compare and contrast. In other words, character development typically occurs as characters not only interact with other characters but are also implicitly evaluated in relation to other characters within the narrative. This effective literary device is illustrated in the narrative portrayals of Saul and David

Setting the Stage

in the Old Testament. In their overlapping stories, readers are confronted with both obvious and subtle differences between the two characters, and they see vivid examples of the consequences of each character's actions throughout the narrative. Indeed, observing how Saul and David contrast throughout the book of 1 Samuel is critical for grasping the overall message of the narrative.

Notice, for example, how the author chooses to introduce each character. When Saul is introduced, he is presented as one who has the conventional features of a king or great man (1 Sam 9:1–2). By all appearances, he will make an ideal future king. Indeed, it is his unique physical traits that even the prophet Samuel points to as he presents Saul to the nation as their new king (1 Sam 10:24). Samuel later operates from the same common human perspective when he sees the appearance of Jesse's oldest son, Eliab, and assumes that this impressive-looking man must be God's choice to be Israel's future king (1 Sam 16:6). God, though, corrects Samuel by telling him, "Do not look on his appearance or on the height of his stature . . . for the Lord does not see as mortals see; they look on the outward appearance, but the Lord looks on the heart" (1 Sam 16:7). This statement, which critiques Samuel's reaction to both Saul and Eliab, sets up the introduction of David. In his case, we find a mere youth, who is handsome, but not on anyone's list of those with potential to be a future king (1 Sam 16:11–13).

By this point in the narrative, we had already been told that God would replace Saul with "a man after his own heart" (1 Sam 13:14). Now we are reminded that God's view of people is different than conventional human views. The narrator thus invites us to compare Saul and David in the narrative that follows to determine what character traits reflect a heart that pleases God. From the very beginning of this process, we find the explicit reminder that physical attributes and human perceptions are meaningless when it comes to those whom God uses to accomplish his purposes. (In fact, those traits that count for much in the wisdom of this world will often hinder people from experiencing God's purpose in their life.) This is clearly illustrated in 1 Sam 17, when Goliath calls for the Israelite army to send out their champion to fight him. Readers expect King Saul to step up to the plate and fight this brute. After all, he is taller by a head than any other warrior in Israel. The story, though, takes an unexpected turn. Saul, a superficially impressive king, shows a distinct lack of courage as he utterly fails to lead the fight for the people of God. Then, David arrives on the scene. He is far smaller than Saul, and apparently not even old enough or impressive enough to be drafted into Saul's service as a soldier. In fact, he was not even supposed to be present at the scene of the looming battle. Notice, though, the striking contrast that his character presents to the character of Saul. David readily accepts Goliath's challenge to battle and demonstrates incredible bravery, trusting in the Lord in contrast to Saul. He does, without hesitation, what Saul *should* have done. Through examining these two characters as a character pair, we discover not only how their outward actions reflect both men's hearts, but we also find that their contrasting actions serve to highlight what it means to be a man after God's own heart.

The New Testament also regularly uses character pairs to communicate narrative meaning. In Luke 10:38–42, for example, we find the story of Mary and Martha who host Jesus and his disciples at a reception in their home. The character of Mary is portrayed sitting at the feet of Jesus, eager to learn from him as he teaches his disciples. The character of Martha, on the other hand, is busy in the kitchen, working hard to prepare a meal that is appropriate for their honored guest, Jesus. It is easy to conclude that Martha is doing something wrong. After all, Jesus gently rebukes her at the end of the narrative. If, though, we were members of that culture, we would quickly recognize that what Martha was doing was exactly what any good hostess would be expected to do. Hospitality is demanded in such situations! And we could point to many Bible verses to support that view. By presenting the two sisters as a character pair, however, Luke makes it clear that there *is* something wrong with Martha's behavior. What she was doing was good, but it was not God's best for her: "But the Lord answered her, 'Martha, Martha, you are worried and distracted by many things; there is need of only one thing. Mary has chosen the better part, which will not be taken away from her'" (Luke 10:41–42). Martha had followed conventional wisdom in making her choice and that conventional wisdom had failed her. It had distracted her from what really mattered. The Savior of the world (John 4:32) was sitting in her living room and she was busy in the kitchen, rather than sitting at his feet.

The contrast between the two sisters provides transparent lessons for modern readers of the story. We quickly recognize that one point of this narrative is that spending time in Jesus' presence is far more important than the busy work that often monopolizes our time. Modern disciples can quickly affirm the common tendency to pour ourselves into ministry at the expense of spending quality time with the Lord. We also discover that what appears to be the right thing to do may not at all be what God

Setting the Stage

wants us to do. And we are reminded that even the commendable features of our culture's values need to be subordinated to the distinct priorities that come from being a disciple of Jesus who lives with the higher values of his kingdom. All of these truths are communicated through the mini-narrative of Mary and Martha that heavily relies on the literary device of a character pair to convey its meaning.

At times, however, modern readers can easily miss instances of character pairs because of how the narrative is structured. In many cases, character pairing occurs without any interaction between the two characters in view. Both Saul and David and Mary and Martha are very directly joined in the narratives in which they appear and are thus naturally read through comparative lenses. At other times, however, contrasting characters appear in their own narrative scenes and readers need to be attentive to features of the narrative that connect the two characters and invite comparison. As we do, we discover that the narrative carries more meaning than we might have initially thought. A good example of this is found in the book of Joshua, where we are introduced to the characters of Rahab and Achan.

We first encounter Rahab in Joshua 2. She is a Canaanite prostitute living in the city of Jericho, which is about to be conquered by Joshua and the nation of Israel. Through a series of surprising events, she and her family are spared when God causes the walls of Jericho to come tumbling down and Israel utterly destroys the city and all its people. This is described in Joshua 6 and is immediately followed by the story of Achan, an Israelite, in Joshua 7. As the Israelites move on from Jericho, they attack the far smaller and less fortified town of Ai. The results, however, are shockingly different than what happened to Jericho. The town of Ai musters a small army that routs the three thousand men that Joshua had sent against them. In the end, we learn that Achan's sin was to blame.

We learn much about the attitudes and actions that please the one true God from reading these two stories. Rahab demonstrates great faith. In fact, her faith is so great and her actions so commendable that they are held up as an example to emulate in Hebrews 11:31 and James 2:25. Achan demonstrates the precise opposite of faith. He treats God as if he doesn't exist. Much could be said about these two characters and the lessons that are taught through their portrayal in the book of Joshua. But something important would be missed if we failed to recognize that the narrator sets them before us as two contrasting characters, as a character pair. If we read each mini-narrative simply on their own terms, we will hear the narrative in "mono," as it were, while if we read them in light of the narrator's character pairing, we will discover that the narrative speaks to us in "stereo."

Think for a moment about what happens when we engage "stereo reading" of the accounts of these two characters. Consider just some of the ways that the narrative contrasts Rahab and Achan. Rahab is a Canaanite woman who should have died with her people, but instead prospered (and became an ancestor of King David and the Messiah; Matt 1:5–6). Achan was an Israelite man who should have lived with his people and prospered, but instead was destroyed like the enemies of God. Rahab's actions led to the survival of her entire family; Achan's actions led to the death of his entire family. Rahab hid the Israelite spies in an act of piety; Achan hid loot that God had forbidden him from taking. Rahab feared the God of Israel even though she had only *heard* reports of what he had done; Achan did not fear God even though he had *witnessed firsthand* the power and goodness of God. The cattle, sheep, and donkeys of Rahab's city perished; the cattle, sheep, and donkeys that belonged to Achan perished. Rahab became *like* an Israelite and lived; Achan became like a Canaanite and died. These contrasts between the two characters are not something that we are creatively reading into the text; the narrative itself invites such comparisons.[22] And the message of Scripture related to these two characters is fleshed out and driven home through these comparisons. As readers read in stereo, they are confronted with the urgency of being like Rahab and taking whatever steps necessary to avoid being like Achan.

As we get into our study of characters in the Gospel of John, we will give particular attention to character pairs in the gospel in order to discover how the narrator makes use of this literary device to help communicate his distinctive message. To grasp that message, though, it is helpful to keep in mind three other major literary strategies that we find utilized throughout the narrative.

Dualism

The Gospel of John presents a distinct dualistic worldview. It contrasts, for example, two domains that stand in opposition: that which is from above and that which is from below. This contrast is driven home, in part, through the dualistic language of light versus darkness, life versus death, and Spirit

---

22. Our analysis here is heavily dependent on Duvall and Hays, *Grasping God's Word*, 296–98.

versus flesh. The domain above is the domain of God. Jesus has come from above to reveal God to the world and to bring people into an everlasting relationship with him. It is from this domain that life, light, truth, the Spirit, and freedom come. The domain below (the world) is the domain of the devil, where death, darkness, falsehood, flesh, and bondage are found.[23]

Characters who encounter Jesus in the Gospel of John are faced with a stark choice that is highlighted through the use of these dualistic themes: accept Jesus and his message by faith and thus enter the domain above or reject him and his message in unbelief and thus remain mired in the world below (cf. 1:11–12). Those who accept the life-giving revelation that Jesus offers are "born from above" (3:3–6; cf. 8:23) and receive eternal life (3:16), while those who reject Jesus and the salvation he offers remain "below" in the dominion of darkness and are already condemned (3:18). In light of this dualistic worldview, being a disciple in the Gospel of John involves (1) being born from above; (2) being part of the realm of the Spirit; and (3) no longer being of this world.[24] Recognizing the dualistic portrayal of life that recurs throughout the Gospel of John will help readers to understand more clearly the lessons on discipleship they encounter through the main characters that appear in the narrative, since many of their choices will be framed in such dualistic language. Indeed, this dualism helps direct readers to expect the characters in the Gospel of John to contrast, as some fall into the categories associated with one realm and others fall into the categories associated with the other realm.

Metaphors

As we examine what the main characters of the Gospel of John teach us about the nature of discipleship, it is also important to read the narrative in light of the metaphors and symbolic language that the apostle John uses to portray Jesus' self-revelation to the world. Both Jesus and the message he brings are described, for example, in terms of light (1:4–5; 8:1; 9:52), water (4:10–11; 7:38), bread (6:33, 35, 51), a gate (10:7), a shepherd (10:11), and a vine (15:1, 5). Each of these christological metaphors, and others, help to clarify the identity and mission of Jesus by using common earthly notions to communicate profound spiritual truths. These metaphors thus

---

23. See Bennema, *Encountering Jesus*, 32.
24. Hillmer, "They Believed in Him," 83.

bridge the heavenly and earthly spheres.[25] As we will see, though, characters who reject Jesus' revelation of the truth, which is often conveyed in metaphorical language, remain mired in confusion and misunderstanding, like Nicodemus who cannot comprehend the meaning of Jesus' reference to the new birth.[26] This leads us to a final feature of John's literary strategy in the Gospel of John.

Misunderstanding

Misunderstanding is a major motif in the Gospel of John. In fact, the characters throughout John's narrative, including Jesus' own disciples, consistently struggle to grasp his identity, mission, and teachings (cf. 2:20; 3:4, 9; 4:31–34; 6:32–35; 8:27; 10:6; 11:13; 12:16; 13:28–29; 20:9).[27] This literary motif is particularly powerful given the knowledge of Jesus' identity and mission that the apostle John provides for readers in the opening verses of his gospel. As *we* read the Gospel of John, we know from the very beginning that Jesus is God in the flesh, who was with the Father "in the beginning" (1:1) and through whom all things were created (1:3). We know from the very beginning that he came to die as the Lamb of God who would take away the sins of the world (1:29, 35). The disciples and other characters in the Gospel of John, however, did not have the benefit of any of this context. So, as they observed Jesus and listened to his teachings in the story world of John's narrative, they had to attempt to reconcile what they were hearing and seeing with both their worldview and with their expectations of what the Messiah would look like. Even Jesus' closest disciples often failed in this effort:

> They fail to understand his reference to Lazarus's death (11:12). Peter misunderstands what Jesus is doing by washing his feet and thus requests a more thorough bath (13:9). Thomas does not understand where Jesus could be going (14:5). Jesus is astounded that Philip could have spent so much time listening to his teaching and observing his actions and still not know him (14:9). The problem,

---

25. See Culpepper, *Anatomy*, 182.

26. John Painter notes that the Johannine symbols effectively "replace the Synoptic parables in the framework of the Gospel. A comparison of the relative functions of symbols and parables highlights this Christological orientation" (e.g., Jesus is the word, the light, the bread, the good shepherd, the vine). Painter, *Reading John's Gospel Today*, 21.

27. Martha's profound declaration of faith is one of the few exceptions (11:27) to this pattern.

> however, goes beyond Peter, Thomas, and Philip; all of the disciples are baffled by Jesus' statements regarding his departure: Some of his disciples said to one another, "What does he mean by saying to us, 'A little while, and you will no longer see me, and again a little while, and you will see me'; and 'Because I am going to the Father'?" They said, "What does he mean by this 'a little while'? We do not know what he is talking about." (16:17–18)[28]

Ultimately, however, by recording the consistent misunderstanding of the disciples and others, the apostle John helps readers of his gospel to grow in *their* understanding of Jesus and his mission. Indeed, "the continual themes of knowledge and lack of knowledge, understanding and misunderstanding encourage readers to think carefully about what is being said so that they *will* understand and know."[29]

In general, misunderstandings in John's Gospel share the following characteristics:

> (1) Jesus makes a statement which is ambiguous, metaphorical, or contains a double-entendre; (2) his dialogue partner responds either in terms of the literal meaning of Jesus' statement or by a question or protest which shows that he or she has missed the higher meaning of Jesus' words; (3) in most instances an explanation is then offered by Jesus or (less frequently) the narrator. The misunderstandings, therefore, provide an opportunity to explain the meaning of Jesus' words and develop significant themes further.[30]

Most of the misunderstandings result from the characters' inability to hear Jesus' words on the metaphorical (spiritual) level he intends. He has "come from above" (3:31; 8:23) so that they can be "born from above" (3:3, 7), but they appear to be stuck in thinking that comes from below. Jesus speaks spiritual truths and they misunderstand them because they are only thinking on an earthly level. Throughout the Gospel of John, though, we see hints of understanding as certain characters show openness to Jesus and his message. Characters who are willing to accept Jesus' revelation and respond appropriately, even with significant gaps remaining in their understanding, move toward knowing the truth and experiencing the life that he offers (8:31–32).

---

28. Culy, *Echoes*, 106–7.
29. Culy, *Echoes*, 107.
30. Culpepper, *Anatomy*, 152.

The motif of misunderstanding, then, will serve a very important purpose in guiding our reading of the Gospel of John. For, the prominence of this motif drives readers to compare and contrast the way in which various characters succeed and fail in understanding who Jesus is and what he is teaching.

Conclusion

In this chapter, we have attempted to set the stage for the stories of various characters that follow. Our goal coincides with the goal of the apostle John in writing his gospel. He has written an engaging account of the life, ministry, and teachings of Jesus not to entertain, but to transform. His goal is faith in Jesus. His goal is eternal life for his readers. His goal is to convince (20:31). And his goal is to spell out, in all sorts of ways, what it means to be a follower of Jesus Christ—a disciple. So, as we proceed to examine significant characters in the Gospel of John, we will encounter qualities of faith and discipleship (or a lack thereof) that are presented to us to imitate (or reject). As we consider various individuals who encounter Jesus, we will see that the choices and opportunities that Jesus presented to them are the same choices and opportunities that are presented to every reader of the Gospel of John. Like the earliest disciples described by John, every reader is confronted by his accounts of Jesus' self-revelation. And particularly through the accounts he provides of key characters, we discover Jesus' invitation to believe in him, to become his disciples, to receive eternal life (3:16; 20:31), and to experience abundant life (10:10) and fullness of joy in this present world (15:11). For that to happen, though, readers today, like the characters in John's account, must wrestle with key questions that the Gospel of John leaves ringing in our ears: "What are you looking for?" (1:38); "Do you also want to become his disciples?" (9:27); "Do you believe this?" (11:26).

Finally, as we begin our character studies in the Gospel of John, we need to remember who the central character of this biographical account is. The primary focus is always on Jesus. It is his identity and mission that is being progressively revealed in each narrative scene we encounter. Although each character and their unique story has value in and of themselves, their stories are ultimately included in the Gospel of John to point readers—indeed urge readers—to a life of faith and discipleship that centers on the person, work, and teachings of Jesus Christ.

2

John the Baptist, Andrew, and Philip

Pointing Others to Jesus

IN MOST OF THE chapters that follow, we will focus our attention on "character pairs," which are made up of two characters that the narrator presents to readers for comparison. As we consider how their actions and attitudes compare and contrast, we will discover important lessons regarding what it means to be a disciple of Jesus. As the narrative proper of the Gospel of John commences in 1:19, however, we discover that the narrator begins with a character *group*. Along with Jesus, the narrative focuses particularly on the actions of three individual characters: John the Baptist, Andrew, and Philip. And, as is sometimes the case with character groups, in particular, the meaning comes not through their contrastive behavior, but through highlighting similarities in their behavior. In other words, the use of multiple characters whose actions are parallel serves to emphasize a particular narrative point as we read the related mini-narratives "in stereo." And the fact that the apostle John uses this literary technique at the very beginning of his narrative proper showcases the importance of this particular narrative point for disciples of Jesus. We encourage readers to take time first to carefully read the passage from Scripture that is in view in this chapter (1:19–51), and in each subsequent chapter, before proceeding.

John the Baptist

Although John the Baptist was introduced in the Prologue in a very limited way (1:6–8, 15), he is the focal character in the first major scene of the

The Making of a Disciple

Gospel of John (1:19–28). Many Jews during John the Baptist's time were eagerly awaiting the Messiah. They were living under the authority of the Roman Empire and many of them felt oppressed. God had given them the land of Israel, but their land was once again controlled by another powerful nation. They were not experiencing the blessings that God had promised to his people in the Old Testament if they lived in obedience to his commands (see Lev 26:3–13 and Deut 28:1–14). They had hope, however, because the Old Testament spoke of a coming Messiah who would deliver them.

When the Jewish authorities came to John the Baptist, they had almost certainly heard rumors that John might be the Messiah. So, they asked him, "Who are you?" (1:19). John quickly set the record straight: "He confessed and did not deny it, but confessed, 'I am not the Messiah'" (1:20). He then went on to point out, in response to their further questioning, that his role was to prepare the way for the coming Lord (1:23). We then find the scene shifting to the next day where John begins to explicitly point others to Jesus: "The next day he saw Jesus coming toward him and declared, 'Here is the Lamb of God who takes away the sin of the world!'" (1:29). In fact, this central aspect of his ministry is showcased through repetition as he again shouts out on the following day: "Look, here is the Lamb of God!" (1:35).

As we see repetition in this passage, or any other, we need to ask: What is the narrator communicating through the repetition? The focus on Jesus as the Lamb of God is obvious, and we will return to that below. But there is other repetition in this passage as well. The passage begins with John the Baptist being a witness of Jesus to the Jewish leaders (1:19–28). In fact, he is the first witness of Jesus in the Gospel of John.[1] The "next day" (1:29), he was again serving as a witness, this time apparently speaking to the crowd around him (1:29–34). The day after that ("the next day," 1:35), he was doing the same thing! God had revealed to John the Baptist that Jesus was the Messiah (1:31–33). And now that he recognized Jesus' identity, what did he do? Day after day, John the Baptist lived to point other people to the Messiah. He watched for every opportunity and was careful to seize it. Crowds of people were coming to him. He could have capitalized on his newfound fame and used it for his own benefit.[2] What, though, did John do with his

---

1. Many scholars have noted that John's Gospel is presented much like a cosmic trial, with witnesses called to bring testimony, signs provided, and evidence given so that when the trial is turned over to the jurors (John's readers), they will be able to receive the whole body of evidence and make a proper decision about Jesus' identity and mission (20:30–31).

2. We learn later in the Gospel of John that many people were acquainted with John

popularity and influence? He pointed the crowds who were drawn to him to Jesus.

Andrew and Philip

What is striking in John 1, however, is that the theme of pointing others to Jesus does not end with the description of the ministry of John the Baptist. As each new character is brought into the narrative, we find them doing the same thing. We are told that one of those who heard John's words was Andrew (1:40). What was Andrew's response to John the Baptist identifying Jesus as the Lamb of God? Not only did he follow Jesus to find out more about him, but after he had spent some time with him, he immediately went and told his brother Peter about Jesus. He pointed Peter to Jesus, just as John the Baptist had pointed him to Jesus. He told Peter, "We have found the Messiah" (1:41). A similar scene unfolds the following day ("the next day," 1:43) as Jesus calls Philip to follow him and Philip in turn goes and tells Nathanael that he has found the Messiah (1:45). Philip came to recognize that Jesus was the Messiah and his response was to point Nathanael to him. Through this character group, then, we see a pattern of people coming to understand that Jesus is the Messiah and then proceeding to tell others about him. So, what specifically do we learn about discipleship from this character group?

Lessons in Discipleship: John the Baptist, Andrew, and Philip

As we look at how John the Baptist responds to the priests and Levites who had been sent to him (1:19), we learn some important lessons about what it looks like to be a disciple of Jesus. What did John do when others thought he might be the Messiah? He was quick to tell them emphatically that he was not the Christ (1:20). He rejected the temptation to allow people to view him as more important than he was. He recognized that life was not about him; it was about doing the work that God had given him to do. To those around him, John the Baptist appeared to be a genuine prophet of God. And the Jews had not seen such a prophet in many, many years. So, in response to John's clear denial about being the Messiah, the priests and

---

the Baptist's testimony about Jesus before they came to believe (10:40–42).

The Making of a Disciple

Levites asked him to explain who he was (1:22). This time John answered by pointing them to the Old Testament (Isa 40:3): "I am the voice of one crying out in the wilderness, 'Make straight the way of the Lord,' as the prophet Isaiah said" (1:23). When John the Baptist was asked about himself, he pointed those who were asking to Jesus instead! He was preparing the way of *the Lord*. He downplayed his own importance in order to highlight Jesus' importance. This is even more evident when the Jewish leaders asked him why he was baptizing, if he was not the Messiah. Look at John's response:

> John answered them, "I baptize with water. Among you stands one whom you do not know, the one who is coming after me; I am not worthy to untie the thong of his sandal." (John 1:26–27)

John does not tell them that he is a great prophet, though he was (see Matt 11:11; Luke 7:28). In fact, he does not claim to be a prophet at all, because he does not want glory for himself or even attention for himself. Instead, John the Baptist points the Jewish leaders to the coming Messiah and tells them that the Messiah is so great that he is not even worthy to be his slave who takes off his shoes (1:27). Readers of the Gospel of John will remember that they have already been told that Jesus, the Word, was not a human being that God had raised up to deliver his people; Jesus was God himself in human flesh. Compared to him even the greatest person in this world is nothing.

John the Baptist was a very important person, but when given the opportunity to have people know how important he was, he used their interest in *him* to point them to *Jesus*. He recognized that not only his role in life but his very identity revolved around serving the Messiah. He existed to prepare people to meet the King of kings and Lord of lords. He existed to serve the Lord Jesus. Like John the Baptist, every disciple of Jesus is called to be careful to give all glory to God. Like John the Baptist, every disciple, and particularly those who serve in ministry roles, must learn to reject the temptation to allow people to put them on a pedestal. Like John the Baptist, every disciple needs to recognize that compared to Jesus, they are lower than the lowest slave. John the Baptist recognized that his life was not about him; it was not about his status, his dreams, his passions, or his agenda. It was about bringing glory to God and pointing other people to the coming Messiah.

If we wonder just how far John's humble devotion to Jesus went, we need not look much farther in the narrative. Look at 1:35–37. Who does John end up pointing to Jesus? Two of his own disciples! He could have encouraged them to continue as his disciples and simply help him point others to Jesus, but he recognized that his whole purpose in life was to help others, including his own followers, to become followers of the Messiah. His goal was not to establish a ministry that would become bigger and bigger. He recognized—as all true disciples will recognize—that his job was to help others to become followers of Jesus, not followers of himself.

Let's pause for a moment and consider some additional lessons from 1:29–34. On the day after his encounter with the priests and Levites, John the Baptist began to publicly point others to Jesus as "the Lamb of God who takes away the sin of the world" (1:29). John's words made it clear that Jesus was not the expected political deliverer that everyone was looking for. In other words, John did not play to the crowds' "felt needs." He did not try to make Jesus more "relevant." He presented Jesus as he was, the Messiah who had come to deliver people from their sins and reconcile them to a holy God. It is very easy for disciples of Jesus today to fall into the trap of thinking they need to package him or package the gospel in a way that will make them appealing to people. John the Baptist models for us the calling of every true disciple. We are to present Jesus to others as God presents him to us in the Scriptures. He is the Messiah who has come to deal with the serious sin problem that all of us have. Jesus came like an innocent lamb to be sacrificed for our sins so that we can be forgiven and have eternal life.

Notice, though, that John also goes on to articulate in detail just how he knew who Jesus was: "I myself did not know him, but the one who sent me to baptize with water said to me, 'He on whom you see the Spirit descend and remain is the one who baptizes with the Holy Spirit.' And I myself have seen and have testified that this is the Son of God" (1:33–34). John's actions here teach us something important about what it means to point others to Jesus. We see two other things in this passage that should characterize the life of every disciple. They not only tell others that Jesus came to deal with their sin problem, but they also (1) explain to others that Jesus is the Son of God. He is not simply a great teacher, a wise man, or an example of how we should treat other people. He existed with God before the world was created; and he was God himself in the flesh (1:1–3, 14). And disciples (2) tell others about their personal experience of Jesus in specific ways. John the Baptist is very detailed as he tells others how he came to recognize that Jesus was the Messiah. Pointing others to the Christ, then, is not simply "showing the love of Jesus" by doing acts of kindness for people.

The Making of a Disciple

Pointing others to the Messiah involves verbally explaining who Jesus is, what he has come to do, and how he has changed our lives.

The lessons we learn about discipleship from the character of John the Baptist in this passage are profound, but in order to drive home the lessons in this chapter, the narrator groups the Baptist with both Andrew and Philip. As we continue through the narrative, we see the same pattern repeated with Andrew and we begin to hear the message in stereo. Look at how Andrew responds when he discovers that Jesus is the Messiah (1:40–42). The first thing he did after encountering the Lord was to go and find his brother Simon and tell him, "We have found the Messiah" (1:41). But that is not all. Andrew *told* Peter that Jesus was the Messiah (1:41) and then *brought* Peter to Jesus (1:42).[3] This is a pattern for every disciple: telling and bringing. It is much like a young man or young woman who is in love. They tell their parents all about the person they have come to love, sharing all of their amazing qualities; but they don't stop there. They are also eager to bring them home to meet their parents. Evangelism is, likewise, about more than conveying information; it is also about *introducing* other people to Jesus.

If we had any doubts about what this narrative is teaching readers, those doubts are removed as we see the same pattern repeated yet again in what follows. Jesus invites Philip to follow him (1:43). Philip not only responds positively to this invitation, but immediately starts behaving as Jesus' disciple. What was the first thing that Philip did as a new disciple of Jesus? He quickly went and told Nathanael that he and others had found the Messiah that the Old Testament had told them to expect: "We have found him about whom Moses in the law and also the prophets wrote, Jesus son of Joseph from Nazareth" (1:45). Notice again, through Philip's words, that pointing others to Jesus involves verbally and substantively explaining to them who Jesus is.

There is more, though, that we learn from Philip about discipleship. When Philip tells Nathanael about Jesus, he gets a less than positive response: "Nathanael said to him, 'Can anything good come out of Nazareth?'" (1:46). At that point, Philip could have concluded: "I guess now is not the time. I don't want to cram anything down Nathanael's throat!" Instead, he did what every disciple should do in most circumstances like this. He invited Nathanael to come and meet Jesus for himself: "Philip said to him, 'Come and see'" (1:46). Although we might have missed it, this is

---

3. See also de Boer, "Andrew: The First Link," 141–43; Bennema, *Encountering Jesus*, 103.

precisely what Jesus had done with Philip. When Philip encountered Jesus, he almost certainly had not only already heard about Jesus and his teachings, but had also seen and heard Jesus himself. So, when Jesus issued the invitation in 1:43 ("Follow me"), Philip immediately responded positively. As one who had been invited, Philip recognized that his new job would be to pass on that invitation to others. And where better to start than with his friend Nathanael? Disciples of Jesus invite others to become disciples of Jesus.[4]

Notice also that the responses to Jesus in this passage reveal some of the features of Jesus' identity and mission that every disciple is expected to embrace. John the Baptist recognizes and embraces Jesus as "the Lord" (1:23), as one who is infinitely greater than he is (1:27, 30), as the sacrifice for sin who would reconcile people to God (1:29, 35), as the one upon whom the Holy Spirit rests (1:32–33), as the one who baptizes with the Holy Spirit (1:33), and as the Son of God (1:34). Andrew recognizes and embraces Jesus as the Messiah (1:41). Philip recognizes and follows Jesus as the Messiah whom Moses and the prophets had foretold would come (1:45). And when Jesus presents Nathanael with a revelation of his power, Nathanael makes the dramatic confession: "Rabbi, you are the Son of God! You are the King of Israel!" (1:49). Disciples today do well to meditate on the significance of each of these aspects of Jesus' identity and mission and ensure that they embrace him as he is revealed in Scripture, rather than popular distortions of the real Jesus.

Lessons in Discipleship: Jesus

We will give more attention in subsequent chapters to what Jesus' actions teach us about discipleship. In this chapter, we will focus on just two. In a sense, in this part of the narrative, Jesus is part of the larger character group we have been considering. In other words, *his* actions reinforce what we are to learn from *their* actions. Notice how Jesus himself models what it looks like to help others come to know him. When he saw two people who were interested in him (1:37), he took the opportunity to invite them to spend time with him (1:38–39). His invitation to "come and see" (1:39) is an invitation to come and personally explore just who he is and what he has come to do. It is an open door into his life. He could have said, "I'm

---

4. We find this message reinforced in a variety of ways as the Gospel of John progresses (see, e.g., 15:27; 17:20).

busy today, but perhaps we can get together sometime." He could have said, "Give me your phone number and I'll contact you when I am free." He could have said, "I'm really tired right now, but perhaps later." Instead, he invited them to come spend the rest of the day with him. He did not let the opportunity pass. Many of us regularly miss opportunities to share the gospel with others because we are not willing to open our lives up to others. We also miss opportunities because we tell ourselves it is not convenient right now to spend time with them. Pointing others to Jesus often involves personal sacrifice.

If we look carefully at our passage, though, we also discover a second lesson about discipleship. Did you notice how Jesus pointed Nathanael to himself? "When Jesus saw Nathanael coming toward him, he said of him, 'Here is truly an Israelite in whom there is no deceit!' Nathanael asked him, 'Where did you get to know me?' Jesus answered, 'I saw you under the fig tree before Philip called you'" (1:47–48). Jesus draws Nathanael to himself by revealing his power to him. He tells him that he saw him while he was still a long way away from him. Only a very mighty prophet or God himself could do such a thing. Nathanael recognized this and said to Jesus, "Rabbi, you are the Son of God! You are the King of Israel!" (1:49). Jesus pointed to himself as the Messiah by revealing his power to Nathanael and Nathanael responded by putting his faith in Jesus. So, what does this teach us about discipleship?[5] It teaches us that we should watch for opportunities where God might want to reveal his power to others, for example, by having us pray for them when they are facing a crisis. If we look at the miracles that God does through the apostles and others in the book of Acts, we find that those miracles were normally done in order to demonstrate God's power to unbelievers so that they would believe the gospel and be saved.

Questions for Disciples

1. Think through all of the ways this passage shows us that we can point others to Jesus. Who does God want you to point to Jesus? Ask God to

---

5. The fact that the character of Nathanael is not even mentioned in the Synoptic Gospels reminds us that each gospel writer was selective in what material he included from the life of Jesus. Here, Nathanael is included in the narrative because his interaction with first Philip and then Jesus serves the apostle John's narrative purpose of creating a character group that will showcase pointing others to Jesus as a central feature of discipleship.

John the Baptist, Andrew, and Philip

show you how you can use the same approaches to introduce others to the Messiah. Start by praying for opportunities to talk to family members, friends, coworkers, or neighbors about Jesus.

2. How might you practice giving glory to Jesus when other people give you honor or attention? In what ways can you take advantage of other people's interest in you or in your accomplishments to point them to the Messiah? What are some examples from your everyday life of how you could follow John's example?

3. Are there people in your life facing some sort of crisis who do not know the Lord? How might you pray for them that God would show his power and presence to them in their circumstances, even as you also tell them about what Jesus has already done for them?

4. Notice again Jesus' response to two "seekers" in 1:35–39. It was the end of the day, and he was almost certainly tired. In what everyday circumstances of your life might you be missing opportunities to invite unbelievers to spend time with you so that you can tell them about Jesus?

5. Philip could have given up when Nathanael seemed to shut down the conversation about Jesus, but he did not. Can you think of times in your own life when you have been too quick to give up when someone did not seem interested in learning about Jesus?

6. Did you notice Andrew's excitement in discovering Jesus and how that excitement led him to want to tell others about Jesus? Have you lost the excitement you had when you first came to know Jesus?

7. When you meet someone new and they say, "Tell me about yourself," how do you respond? Do you highlight your accomplishments? Do you tell them how important your job is? Do you tell them what sports team you root for? John the Baptist did not point to himself at all, though he was a very important prophet! What would happen if you responded by saying, "I am a follower of Jesus Christ"?

8. Read John 1:19–51 again. What other lessons might you learn from the characters in this part of the narrative?

3

Nicodemus

A Confusing Encounter with Jesus

THE FIRST CHARACTER PAIR we will be examining is introduced early in the Gospel of John and both characters play a very important role not only in revealing more of Jesus' identity, but also in revealing more about the nature of discipleship. Read individually, the accounts of Nicodemus and the Samaritan woman each reveal important lessons for disciples today. The fact that the apostle John has chosen to present these two stories side by side, however, invites us to compare the responses of these two characters to Jesus, much like the contiguous stories of Rahab and Achan in the book of Joshua. And John strengthens the connections between the two accounts by using some of the main themes in his gospel to link them (e.g., water, Spirit, eternal life, and witness/testimony). Read together, "in stereo," significant additional layers of meaning become apparent from this character pairing. By analyzing each character's behavior and response to Jesus, readers are better equipped to understand who Jesus is, what discipleship looks like, and what is required to become a devoted follower of the Messiah. We will examine the character of Nicodemus in this chapter, before turning to the Samaritan woman in the next chapter.

The story of Nicodemus spans almost the entire Gospel of John as he shows up in John 3, 7, and 19. The introduction of Nicodemus in John 3 actually begins in the preceding transitional passage:

> When he was in Jerusalem during the Passover festival, many believed in his name because they saw the signs that he was doing. But Jesus on his part would not entrust himself to them,

because he knew all people and needed no one to testify about anyone; for he himself knew what was in everyone. (John 2:23–25)

In 2:23–25, John alludes to signs that Jesus had performed in Jerusalem and the result of his signs: People began to follow him (2:23). We have already been told earlier that "to all who received him, who believed in his name, he gave power to become children of God" (1:12). So, we are surprised to read that Jesus refused to entrust himself to some who "believed in his name." He refused to embrace them as his disciples. How can that be? On the one hand, we are told that Jesus did this because "he himself knew what was in everyone" (2:25). This, of course, leaves us asking the question: What exactly is "in man" that would make Jesus reject a potential disciple? And the apostle John answers that question for us by recounting the story of Nicodemus in what immediately follows in 3:1–21.

Notice how the two passages are connected. Although there is some variation in how the end of 2:25 is translated (NRSV: "for he himself knew what was in *everyone*"; NIV: "for he knew what was in *each person*"), the Greek text more formally reads, "for he himself knew what was in *man*." This is important because the very next words are: "Now there was *a man* of the Pharisees named Nicodemus, a leader of the Jews. This one came to him by night" (3:1, our translation). In other words, our initial impression as readers should be that the apostle John is going to give us an example of the type of "man" to whom Jesus refused to entrust himself (2:25).

How is Nicodemus then described? Nicodemus is the type of person who recognized that the signs Jesus performed communicated something important about his relationship with God: "Rabbi, we know that you are a teacher who has come from God; for no one can do these signs that you do apart from the presence of God" (3:2). He "believed" in the same sense that those described in 2:23 had believed. But we have already been told that such belief is not enough for Jesus. It is not sufficient for such people to be given power to become children of God (1:12). Jesus did not entrust himself to such people (2:24). Nicodemus, at this stage of his relationship with the Messiah, represents those who are impressed by Jesus' signs, but whose faith is inadequate. Although Nicodemus expresses his amazement at Jesus' ability to perform miracles and recognizes him as a teacher who has come from God, he is not yet ready to embrace Jesus for who he truly is and appears incapable of grasping the full significance of Jesus' signs, which reveal the glory of the Father's only Son (1:14; 2:11).

The Making of a Disciple

Light and darkness are very important symbols in the Gospel of John. The fact that Nicodemus comes to Jesus "by night" (3:1) suggests his current spiritual condition corresponds to his lack of initial openness to the truth that Jesus reveals.[1] We might say that he comes out of the darkness of unbelief and into the light for a passing moment to question Jesus before returning again to the darkness from which he had come, though his departure is not actually recorded. The important symbolic language here points us back to 1:5, where we were told, "The light [that Jesus brings] shines in the darkness, and the darkness did not overcome it." The final part of that verse can also be translated "and the darkness has not *understood* it."[2] John seems to delight in using words with double meanings. So, even though the focus in 1:5 is likely on the inability of the darkness to overpower the light, when John returns to the theme of darkness in 3:1, we are not surprised to find a lack of understanding associated with the darkness (3:9–10). Nicodemus thus becomes an illustration of the darkness being unable to "understand the light."

It is important to recognize that although Nicodemus is a singular character, he represents a group: Jewish leaders (3:1). This is confirmed by Jesus' response to him in 3:12: "If I have told you (plural) about earthly things and you (plural) do not believe, how can you (plural) believe if I tell you about heavenly things?" (3:12). Although the conversation is between Jesus and Nicodemus, Jesus uses Nicodemus to make a broader point. He has spoken to the leaders of Israel ("you" plural) and they have refused to accept him for who he was. We thus find what we read at the beginning of the Gospel of John coming true: "He came to what was his own and his own people did not accept him" (1:11). Those who were the most well-versed in the Scriptures refused to believe in the Messiah of Israel.

Scholars agree that Nicodemus was a rabbi and high-ranking leader among the Pharisees, quite likely even a member of the Sanhedrin (7:45–52). He was thus an elite member of Jewish society. His superior credentials produce significant irony in John's account as Nicodemus not only questions Jesus, like a pupil questioning a teacher, but cannot seem to understand what Jesus says to him about the kingdom of God and the new birth "from above" (3:3). Nicodemus is baffled by what Jesus says about how to enter the kingdom of God. In fact, the expression Jesus uses about the new

---

1. John's use of the dualism of light and darkness (or night) can be seen throughout the gospel (cf. 1:4–5, 9; 9:4; 11:10; 13:30; 21:3).

2. See the use of the same verb in Acts 10:34.

birth in 3:3 is ambiguous. It could mean either born "from above" or born "again." This ambiguity, though, is not all that leads to the confusion in Nicodemus, who despite his scholarly credentials is shown to have a very limited understanding of the nature of God's kingdom. Jesus tells Nicodemus that being born from above/again, or being born of the Spirit, is required for a person to enter the kingdom of God. Jesus was teaching Nicodemus a profound spiritual lesson, but Nicodemus was thinking purely in human terms. He heard the expression, "born from above/again," and questioned how a grown man could reenter his mother's womb to be reborn (3:4)! This reaction not only continues to reveal misunderstanding, but it very well may have been a way of deflecting attention from the implications of what Jesus was saying. Like many of us, when confronted by something that makes us uncomfortable, Nicodemus appears to make a cynical comment in an effort to dismiss what Jesus had said and avoid further discussion. But Jesus does not let him off the hook.

If Nicodemus struggled with the idea of being born from above/again, he is even more confused as Jesus transitions into the need to be "born of water and Spirit" to enter the kingdom of God (3:5). He can only hear Jesus' words at a surface or earthly level and continually misses the Lord's metaphorical/spiritual meaning. His final exasperated question to Jesus' revelation shows his total lack of comprehension: "How can these things be?" (3:9). Like his earlier question about a man reentering his mother's womb (3:4), this question is again dismissive. Nicodemus is not humbly asking Jesus to take more time to explain these spiritual truths to him. Instead, he is dismissing them. "How can these things be?" essentially communicates, "No way!" or "That's ridiculous!" Jesus, in turn, tells Nicodemus that what is really ridiculous is that such a learned man is not be able to grasp what he was saying about the kingdom of God: "Are you a teacher of Israel, and yet you do not understand these things?" (3:10).

Notice again the rich irony in this passage, as Nicodemus's encounter with Jesus comes full circle at the end. This Jewish leader who began the conversation by telling Jesus, "*we know* you are a teacher who has come from God," has now proven how little he really knows. Despite his initial confession of recognizing Jesus as a teacher God had sent, he has no idea what Jesus is talking about (3:2, 9). The one who claimed to know has been exposed as one who does not comprehend. The "teacher of Israel" shows himself to be a very poor student!

As we saw in chapter 1, misunderstanding is a major motif in the Gospel of John. Jesus repeatedly reveals his glory and people repeatedly misunderstand who he is and what he has come to do. Even Nicodemus, despite being one of the most respected Bible scholars in Israel, is seemingly incapable of understanding basic truths about the kingdom of God. He is one who thinks "from below," so he interprets Jesus' words from an earthly perspective. He cannot grasp spiritual truths because he has not yet embraced Jesus as more than just "a teacher who has come from God" (3:2). Nicodemus is not yet willing to accept what Jesus says as true (3:11). So, he is not prepared to learn spiritual lessons (3:12) that can only be learned when someone comes to the Lord prepared to embrace and act on what he says. Jesus has come to bring eternal life (3:15), but the way that he will do that is through being "lifted up" on a cross, just as God had brought deliverance in the past through the lifting up of the serpent in the wilderness (3:14; see Num 21:4–9). It had always been God's plan to give his Son, as an act of love for the world, so that "everyone who believes in him may not perish but may have eternal life" (3:16).

With all that Jesus said to him, even holding out to him the offer of eternal life, there is no record at this point in John's account that Nicodemus responded positively to what he heard. Instead of choosing to believe and follow Jesus, Nicodemus apparently leaves without embracing the incredible offer of salvation that Jesus had presented to him. When Jesus, the Light, came into the world, he offered illumination to all people. And he continues to do so. Yet, for fear that their evil deeds will be exposed, most people prefer hiding in the darkness, rather than coming into the Light (cf. 3:19–20).

Lessons in Discipleship: Nicodemus in John 3

Although Nicodemus at this point does not yet embrace Jesus, there are some valuable points about discipleship that we can discover from this account and a few important practical issues that mentors should be aware of when discipling others. First, although Nicodemus's choice to come to Jesus in the dark of night (3:2) symbolizes his lack of spiritual life, it also reveals a desire to come to the light and find out more about who Jesus is and what message he brings. No other Pharisees accompanied him to meet with Jesus; he came alone and for his own reasons, despite the fact that it would have been very bad for his reputation if other Jewish leaders had found out about his meeting with Jesus. So, we should see Nicodemus as a "seeker" in this passage, even though he apparently leaves and returns to the darkness without having grasped or embraced what Jesus was teaching. His example reveals that although people may be attracted to the life Jesus offers, they are often fearful of what others will think and thus try to hide their exploration of Jesus and his teachings. Jesus came to bring light to dark lives, but those who would be his disciples and receive the life he offers must choose to abandon the darkness (3:19–21).

Second, the story about Nicodemus reveals that even though a person may be of a higher social class and well-educated, such qualities do not provide any advantages for receiving what Jesus offers. In fact, status, money, and education are often serious obstacles for someone to put their faith in Jesus. Why? Because the kind of belief that the Gospel of John puts forward for our consideration is belief that leads to humbly embracing both Jesus and his teachings on *Jesus'* terms. It involves letting Jesus define what truth is, rather than continuing to live under our own authority and by what we think is right.

As a teacher of the Jews who had, at least superficially, dedicated his life to the study and the pursuit of God, Nicodemus should have been the most likely person to understand what Jesus revealed about the new birth. But there is no indication that he grasped what Jesus said at all! The irony of this illustrious teacher being unable to understand Jesus' teachings should serve as a powerful warning to all those who see themselves as highly educated or theologically enlightened. Nicodemus no doubt had a well-developed theology, but he missed out on the new birth Jesus offered him precisely because what Jesus revealed did not fit within his theological system. His preconceived notions of how God should work, that is his theology, hindered him from receiving the life that the Messiah offered him.[3] Unfortunately, there are many people like Nicodemus today who scrupulously follow religious doctrines and traditions and yet remain closed to the revelation of the gracious gift of eternal life through Jesus Christ.

Lessons in Discipleship: Jesus in John 3

Nicodemus is certainly not the only character in this account. The central character, of course, is Jesus himself. And just as we learn critical lessons

---

3. His "theological skill becomes an impediment to Nicodemus' ability to become a disciple." Burge, *John*, 125.

related to discipleship from Nicodemus's actions and their consequences, so also we learn critical lessons from Jesus. First, notice how Jesus responds to this "seeker." We might have expected Jesus to say to himself, "I've got a live one here. In fact, this is a mighty big fish among the Jewish leaders. I don't want to let him get away. So, I had better gently reel him into the kingdom." Or, we might have expected him to work hard to establish a relationship with Nicodemus, perhaps asking him about his family or inviting him to be his guest for a nice meal. But Jesus does neither of those things. While God will often lead disciples of Jesus to work hard at relationships with non-disciples before presenting them with the message of the gospel, modern disciples should be open to "cutting to the chase" and addressing the real issues without further ado in some situations, just as Jesus did with Nicodemus. Nicodemus was not some individual who knew nothing about God and needed to be gently led along toward understanding who God is and what God's plan is for the people of this world. Nicodemus likely knew Scripture just about as well as anyone in his day. He needed to grapple with the fact that he was not a member of the kingdom of God. He needed to be confronted with the truth, "no one can see the kingdom of God without being born from above" (3:3), so that he could begin wrestling with the implications of that truth for his own life. Practically, then, disciples of Jesus need always to be seeking to discern where those with whom they interact are at in their understanding of God and his ways so that they can respond in an appropriate way.

Second, the *way* that Jesus responds to Nicodemus forces him to think. In other words, he doesn't say, "Just repeat these words after me, Nick, and you will enter the kingdom of God." He does not make entering the kingdom of God easier than God makes it. He confronts Nicodemus with the fact that (1) he is currently *not* a member of the kingdom of God; and (2) entering the kingdom requires a radical change of life, a change that is so radical that it can be described as a rebirth.

Third, Jesus does not hesitate to rebuke this seeker for his slowness in grasping and embracing the truth. Again, he is less concerned about potentially "letting this one get away," than about making sure that Nicodemus is wrestling with what he has said. The question, "Are you a teacher of Israel, and yet you do not understand these things?" (3:10), is essentially a way of saying, "Get with it, Nicodemus! You ought to know better! Go and think about what I have said to you and you will see that it is all true." Jesus is quite willing to shame this well-respected teacher in an effort to push him toward the front door of the kingdom of God.

When disciples today encounter someone who is interested in Jesus, they often face the temptation to water down Jesus' message so that the person doesn't "get away." Jesus, though, does nothing of the sort. He responds to someone who shows interest in him with the message of life. In other words, he confronts Nicodemus with the truth that speaks to his need, rather than telling Nicodemus what he wants to hear. Jesus is not interested in followers who come to him on their own terms (2:23–25). To become Jesus' disciple, one must embrace the truth. Those who are about the business that Jesus has given them (making disciples), therefore, will be intent on communicating the truth that must be embraced to enter and flourish in the kingdom, rather than on making people feel good about themselves or making people like them. Speaking the truth is acting in love; anything less can never claim to be genuinely caring for the person who does not yet follow Jesus or is struggling to live as his disciple.

Nicodemus: From Darkness to Light

The good news for Nicodemus was that his story was not over. He shows up two more times as the narrative of the Gospel of John unfolds. In John 3, we were left with his question ringing in our ears: "How can these things be?" (3:9). Nicodemus was clearly shocked by what Jesus had said to him. We were not told that he rejected Jesus' words; we were only left with the impression that he went away with much to ponder. We wonder whether he will continue to hide in the shadows or come out into the light as a follower of Jesus. We wonder whether he will remain in the darkness of his own religious and earthly mindset or will embrace the truth that Jesus had revealed to him. The apostle John answers these questions for us by bringing Nicodemus back into the narrative in John 7 and John 19.

In John 3, we saw Nicodemus drawn to Jesus, but unwilling to become his open follower. He appears to remain confused by Jesus' teachings about the kingdom of God and unwilling to commit to becoming his disciple. His openness to Jesus, though, grows over time. When we next encounter him in 7:45–52, we find him taking a baby step out of the darkness and toward the light. The crowds in Jerusalem had begun to openly think that Jesus might, in fact, be the Messiah whom they had been waiting for (7:31). So, the Jewish authorities responded by sending the temple police to arrest him

(7:32). The temple police, however, were too impressed with Jesus' teaching to carry out their assignment. And as they returned to the Jewish authorities, we encounter the character of Nicodemus once again:

> Then the temple police went back to the chief priests and Pharisees, who asked them, "Why did you not arrest him?" The police answered, "Never has anyone spoken like this!" Then the Pharisees replied, "Surely you have not been deceived too, have you? Has any one of the authorities or of the Pharisees believed in him? But this crowd, which does not know the law—they are accursed." Nicodemus, who had gone to Jesus before, and who was one of them, asked, "Our law does not judge people without first giving them a hearing to find out what they are doing, does it?" They replied, "Surely you are not also from Galilee, are you? Search and you will see that no prophet is to arise from Galilee." (John 7:45–52)

Notice the context here. This was a gathering of the chief priests and Pharisees. They were the religious authorities in Israel. They were the Bible experts. And they rejected Jesus as the Messiah. Not only that, they treated anyone who would presume to embrace Jesus as the Messiah as a deceived fool who was ignorant of God's Word and accursed. The apostle John records a key question that the Jewish leaders ask: "Has any one of the authorities or of the Pharisees believed in him?" (7:48). Careful readers have been wondering that very thing since reading of Nicodemus's encounter with Jesus in John 3. Had Nicodemus believed? This passage does not resolve that question, but it does tell us that he had at least come to a point where he was willing to defend Jesus to a limited degree (7:50–51). This suggests that he had been pondering what Jesus had revealed to him earlier and was on his way out of the darkness at this point in the narrative.

There is, though, still one more part to the story of Nicodemus. At the end of the account of Jesus' life and ministry, we find Nicodemus finally coming out fully as a follower of Jesus. He is finished with the darkness and ready at last to walk in the light. Jesus had been betrayed, nailed to a cross, and had died. His followers had deserted him in his hour of need. They should have been the ones to come and take his body and give him a proper burial, but they were overcome with fear. Who would show kindness to Jesus by honoring him in his death? As the apostle John answers that question, he also resolves the question of where the character of Nicodemus stands in his commitment to Jesus at the end of his story:

Nicodemus

> After these things, Joseph of Arimathea, who was a disciple of Jesus, though a secret one because of his fear of the Jews, asked Pilate to let him take away the body of Jesus. Pilate gave him permission; so he came and removed his body. Nicodemus, who had at first come to Jesus by night, also came, bringing a mixture of myrrh and aloes, weighing about a hundred pounds. They took the body of Jesus and wrapped it with the spices in linen cloths, according to the burial custom of the Jews. Now there was a garden in the place where he was crucified, and in the garden there was a new tomb in which no one had ever been laid. And so, because it was the Jewish day of Preparation, and the tomb was nearby, they laid Jesus there. (John 19:38–42)

First, we are introduced to a new character, a secret disciple of Jesus, named Joseph of Arimathea. Up until this point, he had been unwilling to openly follow Jesus because of his fear of the Jews (19:38), but strangely, with Jesus' death, he is now ready to show his allegiance to him. Going to Pilate with a request for Jesus' body was a very public action. Word would have quickly spread to the Jewish leaders that Joseph had sided with Jesus and his followers and Joseph could have expected persecution from his fellow Jews to quickly follow. Then, we read some simple but profound words in 19:39: "Nicodemus, who had at first come to Jesus by night, also came." Where did he go? He went to the cross where Jesus' body was hanging. The flow of the narrative clearly suggests that he, like Joseph of Arimathea, had been a secret disciple of Jesus up until this point.[4] Now, though, he comes to a place that could not be more open to public scrutiny, the cross, and he boldly identifies himself with Jesus.

The extravagant amount of spices used to entomb Jesus' body (19:39) suggests that Nicodemus had come to a deeper understanding of Jesus' identity as King, since such large amounts appear to have been typically reserved for royal burials.[5] Thus, Nicodemus's final actions as a character

---

4. Earlier in John's narrative, readers had been told, "Nevertheless many, even of the authorities, believed in him. But because of the Pharisees they did not confess it, for fear that they would be put out of the synagogue; for they loved human glory more than the glory that comes from God" (12:42–43). Both Nicodemus and Joseph may have been in this category at this point in the narrative, though Joseph is presented as fearing the Jews rather than fearing the loss of human glory. Either way, Nicodemus's lack of open association with Jesus is portrayed as an unresolved black mark on his character until the end of the Gospel of John. As Hillmer rightly notes, the true disciple, "the one who has real faith, must be open in acknowledging Jesus, whereas secrecy only shows that the crypto-disciple does not truly believe." Hillmer, "They Believed in Him," 84.

5. Cf. Keener, *Gospel of John*, 2.1163; Josephus, *Antiquities* 15:61; 17:199.

in the Gospel of John suggest that he has not only come to understand who Jesus is and what he offers, but he has also become Jesus' disciple. The one who initially came to Jesus in the darkness of unbelief is now openly serving the King in the light. His baby steps of open devotion to Jesus in John 7 have given way to full-fledged allegiance to Jesus in John 19 in what is essentially a public confession of his faith as he lavishly buries King Jesus.[6]

Characteristics of Discipleship: The Growth of Nicodemus

As we look at the entire narrative of the Gospel of John, then, we find that Nicodemus represents someone who "gets it" over time. As readers, we do not know what happens to Nicodemus after the resurrection. The Gospel of John concludes his story with the burial of Jesus. Yet, in each scene where the character of Nicodemus appears, we see progression in his commitment to Jesus and his teachings. Indeed, we might say that Nicodemus progresses from doubter (3:1–10) to defender (7:50–51) to disciple (19:38–42). So, the character of Nicodemus, who at first seems easily to fit into a negative category exhibiting traits that should be rejected, becomes a character who is willing to change and who ultimately becomes a positive model of discipleship. He represents one who at first doubts either the need for salvation or Jesus' ability to offer salvation. Or perhaps he simply needs more time to process Jesus' teachings. Eventually, though, he embraces the message of Christ as he comes to understand that Jesus is "the way, the truth, and the life" (14:6). He is thus a character who begins in unbelief, confusion, and rejection of Jesus, but ends with faith, understanding, and acceptance of Jesus. And by presenting this story of transformation, the apostle John invites his readers to recognize that those who initially reject Jesus may well embrace him as they contemplate Jesus' revelation over time.

It is easy for disciples today to become frustrated with the lack of positive response when they tell others about Jesus. They might feel like they are beating their heads against the proverbial wall as they work hard to preach, teach, and live lives that reflect the gospel. The account of Nicodemus's growth in understanding, though, reminds us that such efforts are not in vain. Although some soil may be rocky and hard, as faithful disciples sow the seeds of the gospel, they must also pray for the Spirit to work in the hearts of people and cause those seeds to take root, grow, and eventually bring forth life. The account of Nicodemus encourages disciples of Jesus

---

6. See the discussion of the burial issue in Culpepper, "Nicodemus," 258–59.

not to give up in their efforts to invite others to enter the kingdom of God, even when many initially might reject their message.

Conclusion

Many readers will sympathize with Nicodemus's slowness to embrace Jesus in John 3. Jesus' miracles show that he is from God, but the message he brings is harder to swallow. Jesus demands that any who would receive life from him must turn their backs on their former life, even if that former life was the life of a highly respected religious leader. Nicodemus appears to struggle to take that leap of faith. Jesus' teachings are shocking. Jesus' teachings are radical. Jesus' teachings defy conventional wisdom. But Jesus' teachings are true. And those who would enter the kingdom of God must do so his way. For his way is the only way. Indeed, he himself is the only way (14:6).

As we watch Nicodemus in John 3, we find that it is very hard for those who are wise by the standards of this world to humble themselves and embrace Jesus as wisdom from God. But we also see something that brings us much hope. Those who struggle with that challenge are often given strength from God to overcome the obstacles to finding life through Jesus. Later in the narrative of the Gospel of John, Jesus will tell other religious leaders, "No one can come to me unless drawn by the Father who sent me; and I will raise that person up on the last day" (6:44). By the end of the story of Jesus' life, we find that God has, in fact, drawn Nicodemus to Jesus and Nicodemus is ready to risk everything that had previously mattered to him in this life in order to serve his new Master (19:39). Those who seek, do find, even when they come from a religious system that appears to be opposed to Jesus and the message he came to bring.

Questions for Disciples

1. Do you know someone who is like Nicodemus, interested in Jesus, but still stuck in their own way of thinking? How might Jesus' model of evangelism help you reach out to that person with the truth of the gospel?

2. Have you assumed in the past that certain people must be followers of Jesus because they believe in God and have a lot of knowledge about

the Bible? How might the story of Nicodemus lead you to think more carefully about that person's spiritual state and need?

3. Do you assume that your knowledge of the Bible or theology makes you spiritually mature? How does the story of Nicodemus correct that thinking?

4. Are there ways in which your own theological commitments or pet doctrines actually keep you from knowing Jesus more deeply, or perhaps knowing him at all?

5. What does "born again" or "born from above" language imply about the change that takes place when someone truly becomes a follower of Jesus? If you're honest, had you tended to view being a Christian as simply adding Jesus (and heaven) to an already good life, rather than starting a completely new life?

6. Is there someone in your life who is a seeker who desperately needs a direct presentation of the truth or a gentle rebuke, rather than simply being "shown the love of Jesus" through your life?

7. Have you spoken the message of the gospel to someone who has not yet responded positively? How does the example of Nicodemus's later life encourage you to continue speaking to and praying for that person to receive Jesus' invitation of life?

4

The Samaritan Woman

A Transformational Encounter with Jesus

IN JOHN 3, READERS were introduced to a great teacher of the law who failed to hear Jesus' words with the ears of faith and remained trapped in the darkness of his ignorance, unable to grasp and embrace Jesus' message about the new birth. Although this is followed by additional teaching about Jesus' mission (3:17–21) and an account of an interaction between some of the disciples of John the Baptist and Jesus (3:22–36), the next major character introduced into the narrative is the Samaritan woman at the well in John 4. Just prior to her introduction, the same themes that were introduced in the account with Nicodemus are reinforced in 3:31–36. Jesus brings testimony from heaven above (3:31), but some people, like Nicodemus, refuse to accept his testimony (3:32). Those, however, who choose to embrace what Jesus says embrace God himself (3:33) and will experience the gift of the Spirit (3:34). Indeed, those who believe in the Son—embracing him and his message fully—receive eternal life (3:36). Nicodemus in John 3 exemplifies those who do not yet accept Jesus' testimony as true. There are others, though, who respond differently and become Jesus' disciples.

In John 4:1–42, we are introduced to a Samaritan woman who not only accepts the revelation Jesus offers but also runs to tell others about him. In comparison to Nicodemus, a respected teacher and leader in Israel, the Samaritan woman was disreputable at best. She had a shady past and was shunned by respectable citizens. As was the case with Nicodemus, her response to Jesus is unexpected. With Nicodemus, we expected him to quickly connect what he saw and heard from Jesus with the Scriptures he knew so well and thus become Jesus' disciple. With a foreigner who had seemingly lived her life with no fear of God, we expected the Samaritan woman to continue in her rebellion. Instead, we see the opposite in both cases. And this shocking contrast teaches us important lessons.

The encounter between Jesus and the woman of Samaria takes place in a cultural setting where there was great disparity between genders, social classes, and racial groups. It was also a time filled with religious tension and bigotry. Any conversation between a Jew and a Samaritan would be rare given the hostility between the two groups.[1] In this episode, however, Jesus is not only speaking with a Samaritan, but dares as a Jewish man to speak to a woman from that despised group. This would have been shocking behavior in that culture. Not only would a Jew not talk to a Samaritan and a man not speak privately to a woman outside of his family, but for a Jewish rabbi to address a Samaritan woman of ill repute would have been almost unthinkable.

It is important to be attentive to details in John's account, including the setting for the story. We are told that Jesus was sitting at Jacob's well at about noon (4:7). And it was at that time that the woman came to draw water (4:7). The conversation that follows is private; no one else was apparently present. What we easily miss is that the Samaritan woman was almost certainly at the well alone at midday because she was shunned by her own people because of her lifestyle and past history.[2] Women of the time would typically draw water in groups in the cooler part of the day. In fact, going to the well and talking together would have been a central part of social life for women. To be excluded from this part of society would have been very difficult for any woman. It is into this dark, lonely existence that Jesus brings light by engaging this despised woman. The Samaritan woman is astonished when Jesus speaks to her and asks her to share some water with him: "How is it that you, a Jew, ask a drink of me, a woman of Samaria?"

---

1. The tensions between Judaeans and Samaritans can be traced back to the time after the death of King Solomon and the division between the Northern Kingdom of Israel, with its capital in Samaria, and the Southern Kingdom of Judah, with its capital in Jerusalem. Following the Assyrian invasion of the Northern Kingdom in 720 BC, and the intermarrying of Samaritans with foreigners, the southern Jews believed the northern Samaritans to be apostates who had become corrupt and impure. As a result of their disdain, the Southern Kingdom rejected any Samaritan assistance in the reconstruction of the temple after the Babylonian exile and the Samaritans responded by establishing a rival temple on Mount Gerizim, which contributed to the longstanding hostility.

2. On the woman's potential moral failings, see Keener, *Gospel of John*, 1:593–96. See also the challenge to this line of thinking in O'Day, "Gospel of John," 565–67.

(4:9). We soon learn, though, that it is Jesus who has something to share with her: "If you knew the gift of God, and who it is that is saying to you, 'Give me a drink,' you would have asked him, and he would have given you living water" (4:10). In Jesus' reply, he introduces both the gift of "living water" and the Giver of that gift.[3]

Intrigued, the woman asks Jesus where she can obtain the living water of which he speaks (4:11). Like Nicodemus, the woman initially misunderstands Jesus' words. She hears about "living water" and thinks at a purely earthly level that Jesus must be talking about flowing water that comes from a spring or a stream.[4] She figures that if she can find this running water, it will make her daily job of acquiring water much easier. Her misunderstanding is reinforced by her reference to both the bucket and the well in 4:11, and also by her question as to how the water offered by Jesus is better than the water that she already draws from the famous well of her ancestor Jacob (4:12).[5]

As in the account of Nicodemus, Jesus is speaking on a spiritual level to a person who is thinking on an earthly, physical level. And as he did with Nicodemus, Jesus continues to flesh out his revelation of spiritual truth to the Samaritan woman: "Everyone who drinks of this water will be thirsty again, but those who drink of the water that I will give them will never be thirsty. The water that I will give will become in them a spring of water gushing up to eternal life" (4:13–14). Here, Jesus informs the Samaritan woman that whereas earthly water temporarily quenches thirst, the heavenly water that he offers fully and forever satisfies one's spiritual thirst by bringing eternal life. Though the woman continues to misunderstand Jesus'

---

3. See Bennema, *Encountering Jesus*, 163.

4. "Living water" and "flowing water" are expressed the same way in Greek.

5. The setting at Jacob's well and the woman's question as to whether Jesus is greater than her ancestor Jacob who built the well (4:12) establish an opportunity to present Jesus as greater than the patriarch Jacob. Jesus bringing something new and greater is a consistent theme throughout John's Gospel. Like the first sign in Cana, where Jesus' new wine replaces the water used for purification, here Jesus' living water now replaces the water of Jacob's well, by providing what Jacob's water cannot, the gift of eternal life; Beasley-Murray, *John*, 58. Because the only water allowed for ritual washings to purify unclean worshipers was "living" or "moving" water, John is once again including the concept of Jesus replacing the Jewish ritual of purification; Burge, *John*, 143. This replacement of Jacob's well is significant to John's readers because of the implication that Jesus and his water are greater than both Jacob and his well; Keener, *Gospel of John*, 1:601. This symbolic comparison reveals that the religious offerings available in Judaism will not truly satisfy, but the living water offered by Jesus provides an everlasting salvation.

spiritual meaning at this point, she remains captivated by the conversation and requests that Jesus give her this water, "so that I may never be thirsty" (4:15). The conversation that began with Jesus as a thirsty traveler requesting well water from a Samaritan woman has now been reversed as the woman requests the living water that only Jesus can provide to quench her thirst.

At this point in John's account, the dialogue takes an unexpected turn. Jesus asks the woman to go fetch her husband (4:16). As we soon learn, Jesus is not just making conversation; he is about to reveal his glory to this despised woman. The Samaritan woman replies that she has no husband (4:17), which in turn leads Jesus to reveal that he knows about the five previous husbands she has had and he knows that the man she is now with is not her husband (4:17–18). Listen to the woman's response: "Sir, I see that you are a prophet. Our ancestors worshiped on this mountain, but you say that the place where people must worship is in Jerusalem" (4:19–20). It is quite possible that the woman's response is intended, like Nicodemus's before her, to move the conversation away from an uncomfortable topic. Or, she may genuinely be interested in hearing how Jesus, who has now revealed himself to be a prophet, would resolve the well-known dispute between Samaritans and Jews about the proper place to worship God (4:20). What is clear is that the woman has taken a step forward in recognizing who Jesus is. He is more than she initially thought him to be; he is a prophet. And a prophet could tell her where and how God wants people to worship him.[6]

Jesus' answer quickly sidesteps the Samaritan woman's theological question and essentially negates any debate regarding the correct place of worship. He tells her that neither the Temple Mount in Jerusalem nor the Samaritan shrine on Mount Gerizim are ultimately where God desires his people to worship him (4:21). Instead, offering new revelation, Jesus informs the woman that since God is Spirit, neither Mount Gerizim nor Jerusalem are important, because they are mere earthly, physical places and the only place to encounter God in worship ultimately is "in Spirit" (4:23). As in the previous story, Jesus challenges earthly thinking with heavenly truth. Rather than relying on ethnic boundaries or religious markers for the worship of the God who is Spirit, those who would properly honor the Father

---

6. Her question revolves around the religious debate between Jews and Samaritans that had divided them for centuries. The Samaritans had built their temple on Mt. Gerizim near Shechem, viewing the Jewish temple in Jerusalem as a rival temple. The woman's question to Jesus about spatial location is essentially, "Who is correct, Jews or Samaritans in their assertions about the place where God is truly worshiped?"

The Samaritan Woman

will do so according to the spiritual truth that is revealed through Jesus (4:24). As Jesus has already revealed that he is the true Temple (2:13–22), the place where God's presence exists on the earth, so now he reveals that true worship can only happen in the Spirit. Genuine worship, then, will no longer be associated with a location. Instead, worship that pleases God will be empowered by the Spirit as Jesus ushers in a new age through his sacrificial death on the cross and his resurrection.

Once again, the Samaritan woman is intrigued by what Jesus is saying and shares her hope that when the Messiah comes he will settle, once and for all, every theological question (4:25).[7] In an incredible statement of self-revelation, Jesus responds to the woman with words that offer the fulfillment of her messianic hope. Using the words of divine self-revelation in Exodus where God proclaims himself to Moses as "I am" (Exod 3:14), Jesus discloses his identity as the Messiah to the woman: "I am he, the one who is speaking to you" (4:26). His choice of words, though, take her beyond her messianic expectations. Jesus essentially tells her, using language that is prevalent in the Gospel of John, "I, who am speaking to you, am the Christ, and the Christ is more than just the Messiah God promised."[8]

When Jesus reveals himself to be the Messiah, the woman accepts his testimony (remember 3:33), drops her water jar, and immediately runs to her city to proclaim to others all that Jesus has revealed to her (4:28–29). Symbolically, the act of leaving her water jar perhaps demonstrates that she has come to recognize Jesus' identity as the bearer and source of the living water, that she is no longer troubled by the mundane need for physical

---

7. The concept of the Messiah in Samaritan thought differed somewhat from the Jewish view. Like the Jews, the Samaritans expected a "prophet-like-Moses," but they did not connect this messianic figure to the Davidic royal line due to the fact that the Samaritans recognized only the Pentateuch, rejecting the Former Prophets and the Prophetic Writings (Josephus, *Ant.* xviii, 85–88). Based on the messianic hopes centered in Deut 18:15, the Samaritans believed that the coming *Taheb* ("Restorer") would declare the words of God and reveal the truths of God.

8. Jesus' many "I am" statements in the Gospel of John likely draw more on "I am" sayings in Isaiah (see 43:10; 45:3, 6, 7; 52:6). Although Samaritans held primarily to their version of the Pentateuch, rather than the entire Hebrew Bible, as their primary Scriptures, the woman may well have been familiar with Isaiah. At the very least, she would have likely had some level of familiarity with the famous dialogue between God and Moses in Exod 3. Ultimately, though, the importance of Jesus' "I am" statement is primarily for readers of the Gospel of John who experience these statements as a central tool in Jesus' revelation of his character and glory. For more on Jesus' "I am" statements in the Gospel of John, see Culy, *Echoes*, 113–17; Ball, *'I Am' in John's Gospel*.

water, and that her thirst has now been quenched with the spiritual water offered by the Messiah.

Notice how the narrative shows us that after recognizing Jesus as the Christ, the Samaritan woman's life was immediately transformed. She could not help but go to the very ones who had shunned her and tell them about Jesus. The woman employs the same testimonial formula, "Come and see" (4:29), in her invitation to the people of her community that Jesus used in calling his first disciples (1:39) and that Philip used in his invitation to Nathanael (1:46). This is a pattern that is developing in the Gospel of John. Disciples who discover Jesus are eager to go and invite others to meet him.[9]

The positive response by the Samaritan community to the woman's testimony, where many come to believe in Jesus (4:39), clearly reveals, if we had not realized it already, that the Samaritan woman is now a disciple and true witness of the Messiah. Her belief and witness that Jesus is the Christ (4:29) leads to their confession that Jesus is the "Savior of the world" (4:42). Indeed, the development of the Samaritan woman's discipleship is reflected in the titles she uses for Jesus throughout the text. She begins by viewing him as "a Jew" and thus an adversary (4:9), progresses to respectfully addressing him as "Sir" (4:11, 15, 19), then acknowledges him as "a prophet" (4:19) before finally concluding that he is "the Messiah" (4:29).[10] The obstacles that would have kept her from experiencing God (her sinful past, her gender, and her ethnicity) were overcome as she embraced what Jesus said about himself to be true.[11] And in a moment, she goes from being a despised sinner to being a disciple who eagerly testifies about Jesus and brings people to him, becoming a conduit of living water for those around her.

Reading in Stereo: Nicodemus and the Woman at the Well

Unlike Nicodemus who approached Jesus in the dark of night, the woman encountered him during the brightest part of the day (4:6). The difference in setting between the two stories likely symbolizes the differences between the characters' openness to what Jesus is offering them. The woman meets Jesus in the light and chooses to remain in the light despite the fact that the light exposes her sinfulness (3:21). In the account of Nicodemus, being

---

9. See also Coloe, "Woman of Samaria," 192.
10. Bennema, *Encountering Jesus*, 168.
11. Keener, *Gospel of John*, 619.

exposed to the light showcases his ignorance about the ways of God and there is no indication that he moved toward the light or remained in the light after his surreptitious encounter with Jesus. In contrast, the Samaritan woman chooses to continue in the light of Jesus' presence and thus receives the living water that he offered. In a sense, she exemplifies the truth of 1 John 1:7 ("if we walk in the light as he himself is in the light, we have fellowship with one another, and the blood of Jesus his Son cleanses us from all sin"), as she not only is transformed by the light herself and cleansed from sin, but also moves from a state of tension with her community to a shared experience of life as she witnesses about Jesus to her community and they too respond with faith.

It is noteworthy that these twin stories also share structural similarities, which help highlight the different hearts of the two characters as both are presented with the same opportunity to accept the revelation that Jesus offers them. Mark Strauss's careful investigation reveals seven parallels between the two episodes. First, a spiritual metaphor is used to spark interest: the new birth and the living water metaphors. Second, having heard Jesus' words, both Nicodemus and the woman misunderstand what Jesus is talking about. Third, Jesus clarifies the spiritual meaning behind his metaphors. Fourth, the two characters become more confused. Fifth, Jesus clarifies again, and this time also offers a mild rebuke. Sixth, Jesus then reveals his identity to them. And seventh, both characters respond: Nicodemus with silence[12] and the woman with enthusiasm.[13] The seventh parallel is the highpoint since it deals with the final reaction to Jesus by the characters. One fails to respond; the other accepts and receives life.

Whereas Nicodemus represents the Jewish religious intellectual class who should have been ready to understand and follow Jesus, the Samaritan woman is a far more unlikely candidate for discipleship. Ironically, while the religious leaders are closed to what is offered (cf. 1:11), a seemingly irreligious woman is open to Jesus and his teachings (cf. 1:12). Nicodemus

12. We want to be very cautious about arguments from silence. We are not actually told *how* Nicodemus responded. We are left wondering. We properly assume that he did not resolve on this occasion how he would respond to Jesus, but that does not mean that he resolved to reject Jesus' offer. It only suggests to us that he was not yet prepared to embrace Jesus and his teachings. By recording no final response from Nicodemus whatsoever, the apostle John effectively highlights even more sharply the difference between Nicodemus and the Samaritan woman who jumps up and runs to tell others about Jesus, the Christ. With Nicodemus, we are left with the final words the apostle John records from his lips: "How can these things be?" These words certainly do not point to belief.

13. Strauss, *Four Portraits*, 302–3.

is not only a Jew, but a man, a member of the wealthy elite, a Pharisee, and a Scripture expert. The Samaritan, on the other hand, is a presumably uneducated woman from a lower social class, the wrong ethnicity, and a rejected outcast even among her own people. Nicodemus had a stellar reputation among his people; the Samaritan woman was so disreputable that no other women in her community would be seen with her drawing water from the well. These dramatic contrasts lend force to the twin stories as we see the one who should "get it" failing to receive life from the Messiah and the one who we would not expect to "get it" becoming Jesus' disciple. One remains in the dark, while the other embraces and enters the light. Reading these two accounts in stereo, then, reminds us that those who are viewed as less valuable by society are often the most willing and eager to receive the living water that Jesus offers. And like the woman, such people are often also the most eager to go out and draw many to Christ not only because they recognize more clearly the amazing thing that God has done for them, but also because the dramatic change in their lives serves as a powerful testimony to the truth of the gospel.

In the end, the account of Nicodemus is an invitation to believe in Jesus, receive the new birth from above, and become his disciple, but it is also a warning that failure to embrace Jesus on his terms will leave one in the darkness. Likewise, the story of the woman at the well is an invitation to receive the Messiah, accept the living water of redemption, and have one's spiritual thirst truly satisfied through becoming a disciple of Jesus. At the same time, it is a reminder of just how far the love and grace of God extend. No one is beyond the reach of God's love and his offer of eternal life through Jesus Christ. All are invited to become Jesus' disciples, but they must come to him on his terms.

Lessons in Discipleship: The Samaritan Woman in John 4

The Samaritan woman presents us with a number of other important lessons on discipleship. First, we see a willingness by the woman to remain in the presence of Jesus, not allowing her checkered past to deter her from what he is offering. She does not walk away from the light even when her sin is exposed. Mature followers of Jesus understand that their ongoing exposure to the light will continue to expose darkness and sin in their lives (3:19–20). In fact, it is fair to say that the closer we get to Christ, the more aware we will become of sins that we had never thought about before in our lives. This is an important part of the process of sanctification, of becoming more like Jesus. Disciples will not hide in darkness, where their sins can remain undetected; they will run to the light and "walk in the light" because they will desire to be purified from all sin (3:21; 1 John 1:7; 3:3). A disciple will cry out like the psalmist: "Search me, O God, and know my heart; test me and know my thoughts. See if there is any wicked way in me, and lead me in the way everlasting" (Ps 139:23–24). The woman's decision to remain in the light even when the light shone upon her dark past illustrates a mark of true discipleship. Although she was likely very uncomfortable by Jesus' revelation of her past sinful life, she persisted in interacting with him and thus received more and more revelation, culminating with Jesus' revelation that he is the Messiah (4:26). The Samaritan woman is thus an example of God rewarding those who diligently seek him (Heb 11:6).

Second, the Samaritan woman shows us that the path of discipleship begins with a teachable spirit. At several points in the conversation, a proud person would have likely gotten up and walked away. Like the Samaritan woman, many people today are trapped in lives of sin or are shunned by society. Others have hearts that are eager to know God, but they allow past mistakes, bad theology, or pride to keep them from drawing near to Christ and finding freedom through him. Like the Samaritan woman, they might have many barriers between them and knowing God, but if they are humble and open to hearing the message of life, they too can find freedom and become a new person. All of this, of course, implies that disciples of Jesus today will be willing and prepared to bring Jesus' living water to those who are thirsty, but distant from God and perhaps even isolated from others.

A third aspect of discipleship is displayed as the woman leaves her old ways (repentance) and fully embraces Jesus and his teachings, which is vividly portrayed as she leaves her water jar behind and races off to tell others about him. Genuine conversion involves embracing the truth *and* acting on that truth in repentance and service to the one true God.[14] The Samaritan woman goes from living for herself and her own desires to serving the Messiah and living for his glory. Her response to Jesus shows that the living water she received from him was more important than any cheap substitute the world or her religion had to offer. The world presents many offerings to distract believers and will try to get them to attempt to quench their thirst with possessions, sex, power, entertainment, or even empty religion. Yet,

---

14. Remember the two features of Paul's description of the Thessalonians' conversion: "you turned to God from idols, to serve a living and true God" (1 Thess 1:9).

Jesus' thirst-quenching revelation that he is what people are longing for still resonates for disciples who know that what he provides surpasses anything that the world can give.

A fourth aspect of discipleship is seen when the woman runs to her city to tell others about Jesus, despite her low status in the community. Disciples know that their sinful past no longer matters. The only thing that now matters is their new life in Christ. "So if anyone is in Christ, there is a new creation: everything old has passed away; see, everything has become new!" (2 Cor 5:17). The woman was quick to tell others about her encounter with Jesus. She did not let the obstacles of past sin or wounds caused by rejection, condemnation, or her own low view of herself keep her from testifying about what Jesus had done for her.

A fifth aspect of discipleship is revealed in the woman's willingness to partner in ministry with Jesus. Her work is supported by Jesus' words to his disciples about fields that are ready for harvest at the end of this narrative (4:35). While the disciples are learning from Jesus' teaching, the woman is already out reaping the ripe fields with the result that many citizens of her city put their faith in him (4:39–41). The meeting between Jesus and the Samaritan woman is an important example of how one encounter can not only impact the course of a single life, but can transform an entire community when that new disciple is willing to be used by God. In fact, the Samaritan woman's actions teach us a profound lesson about evangelism that we dare not miss. Who does God intend to use to spread the Good News of Jesus Christ to our neighborhoods and to the nations? Everyone who is a genuine disciple of Jesus! This woman with a notorious past did not try to convince others to listen to her. She did not take years to attempt to rebuild her reputation. She simply spoke the truth that Jesus had revealed to her and God changed the lives of many in her town. This should remind us that it is the *gospel* that God uses to powerfully save people (Rom 1:16), not our ability to convince, our good reputation, or even our ability to build relationships. All of those things may be helpful and often even reflect the way that God chooses to work, but they are not *necessary* for God to save anyone. The only thing that is necessary is that people hear the biblical gospel. That is what God uses to save people. For the Samaritan woman, the end result of all of this was that this marginalized woman undoubtedly gained a new status in her community as she became the conduit through whom living water was brought to her village.

The Samaritan woman reminds us that the most natural response to becoming a genuine disciple of Jesus is to want others to know him as well. We cannot understand the gospel and be apathetic about the plight of others who have not yet heard. We cannot believe that "Whoever has the Son has life; whoever does not have the Son of God does not have life" (1 John 5:12) and fail to care about those who do not have the Son. By its very nature, receiving eternal life as a new follower of Christ implies that we will engage in evangelizing others so that they too can have eternal life. Truly coming to know Jesus necessarily creates in a new disciple a desire and urgency for others to know him too. Too often, modern disciples are so busy trying to live their own lives and meet their own needs, like Jesus' disciples in this episode, that they miss important opportunities to witness to lost and thirsty people around them. Opportunities present themselves, but disciples must be ready and willing to have a conversation about the living water that flows in and through their own lives (cf. 7:37–39).

Finally, if we look at the Samaritan woman's questions, we find a good sampling of the sorts of questions that spiritually thirsty people around us are still asking today: "Why would you talk to me?" "Where does this living water come from?" "Are you greater than my religious traditions?" "What is real worship?" "Who is the Messiah?" It is essential that disciples of Jesus be ready with satisfying answers to such questions that are grounded in the Word of God so that people can continue to receive the thirst-quenching living water that Jesus offers. "Always be ready to make your defense to anyone who demands from you an accounting for the hope that is in you" (1 Pet 3:15).

Lessons in Discipleship: Jesus in John 4

In addition to these lessons that we learn from the Samaritan woman's actions, we also learn a number of important lessons about discipleship from the actions of Jesus in this passage. First, we vividly see the extent of God's love for the people of this world displayed. In the Father's eyes, those whom society despises are lost sheep who need to be rescued. Just as Jesus was eager to bring the message of life to this shunned woman, so too we should be watching for those who are shunned by society and be quick to bring them the offer of living water. Jesus consistently demonstrated his willingness to reach out to people who were viewed as the dregs of society. He became famous for hanging out with "tax collectors and sinners," which would have had a very similar connotation to "drug dealers and prostitutes" in our context. In John 4, we see Jesus' willingness to set cultural expectations aside for the sake of reaching a needy, foreign, sinful woman with his life-changing message. There were a thousand reasons why Jesus should have avoided a conversation with this woman, but he rejected them all. Why? Because he saw a person in need and he had come to earth, as the Word who became flesh, precisely to meet such needs. All of this should remind disciples of Jesus today that we dare not let cultural expectations or any sort of prejudice keep us from taking the good news to every kind of person in our community and throughout the nations. There are thirsty people everywhere who look, sound, think, talk, and may even smell different than us, but who need to hear of God's love for them.

Second, we see that Jesus takes the initiative to engage this needy woman. Far too often, Christians insist that they would tell others what Jesus has done for them if God would only give them opportunities. Instead, disciples should see every encounter with someone new as an opportunity to try to start a spiritual conversation in natural and creative ways. The mundane situations of everyday life regularly provide us with such opportunities, if we will only open our eyes to see them. Jesus reminds us through his actions that opportunities to engage people with the message of life can be created, if we are willing to take the initiative.

Third, Jesus' engagement with the Samaritan woman should remind us that delivering the message of life requires confronting the problem of sin. Jesus did not gloss over the woman's promiscuous past or present, because people who do not recognize the bad news of their sinful state can never embrace the good news of what God has done for them. True love does not pretend that sin does not exist. True love is not helping people feel good about themselves. True love diagnoses the deadly disease of sin and then offers the prescription that will bring new life and health.

Fourth, when faced with a common theological debate that could easily move him away from what he wanted to say to this woman, Jesus did not take the bait. Instead, he quickly defused the debate ("neither on this mountain nor in Jerusalem," 4:21) and then focused on revealing the truth that the woman needed to hear. Disciples need to learn to focus on what really matters and not get tricked by the evil one's schemes into conversations that will only lead to arguments and strife, rather than leading to life.

Fifth, Jesus intentionally talks to the woman on her level. He did not speak over the Samaritan woman's head and he did not speak in a way that made her feel ignorant. If we love one another and if we love those who do not yet know the Lord, we will speak in language they can understand.

Sixth, Jesus showed genuine interest in the Samaritan woman. He did not just greet her; he willingly had an extended conversation with her in which he got to know her story and her current need. While developing a deep relationship may not be necessary for sharing the gospel with people, anyone who is going to listen to us needs to see that we genuinely care about them. They do not want to feel like a project or someone we are just trying to convert. They need to see that we value them as a person. Just as followers of Jesus need to be prepared to bring spiritual answers to the deep questions that people have, so also they need to be careful to speak in an appropriate way. Look at what follows the verse we referred to above from 1 Peter 3: "Always be ready to make your defense to anyone who demands from you an accounting for the hope that is in you; *yet do it with gentleness and reverence*" (1 Pet 3:15–16). Jesus beautifully illustrates both readiness and gentleness.[15]

Conclusion

Careful attention to detail in each of these episodes reveals numerous lessons for modern disciples. When we recognize, though, that Nicodemus and the Samaritan woman are presented as a character pair in the narrative and we read their narratives in stereo, those lessons are driven home and fleshed out further. The striking contrast in their responses to Jesus helps highlight what is at stake as we and others encounter the Messiah and his message of life. Surprisingly, the twin narratives encourage us to be more like the shunned, disreputable Samaritan woman than like the highly respected Jewish Bible scholar. We are reminded, then, that when it comes to those who will enter the kingdom of God, appearances can be deceiving. Indeed, appearances and past history are irrelevant. The message of life that Jesus brings is a message for all. Those who embrace it, though, must set aside their preconceived notions and embrace him on his terms. The Samaritan woman did just that, and ultimately so did Nicodemus. Their responses to Jesus invite us to respond to him and his teachings in the appropriate way, and help others to do the same.

---

15. The reference to "reverence" in 1 Pet 3:16 likely refers to the "fear" of the Lord, which will lead disciples to answer in a manner that honors God and is consistent with his character.

THE MAKING OF A DISCIPLE

Questions for Disciples

1. Do you know someone who is despised like the Samaritan woman or who seems beyond the reach of God's love? How might Jesus' model of evangelism help you reach out to that person? How might Jesus' example lead you to watch more carefully for such people in your everyday life? What sorts of people does your society treat like the Samaritan woman?

2. Jesus became exhausted just like you and I become exhausted. Have you ever used weariness as an excuse for failing to reach out to someone in need?

3. Do you see every interaction with a stranger as a potential opportunity to tell that person about the Messiah? Do you, like Jesus, take the initiative and try to start spiritual conversations with others who may not know him?

4. Are you afraid to talk about sin with those who do not know Jesus? Have you fallen into the trap of thinking someone can embrace the Good News without first acknowledging the bad news of their sin problem?

5. Are you more concerned with theological debates than with helping others to enter the kingdom of God? What are some of the modern denominational differences (distinctive beliefs) that cause unnecessary division among Christians and perhaps distract us from helping others to know Jesus?

6. How does the Samaritan woman's evidence of new birth compare to the evidence in your own life? If someone wrote an account of your encounter with Jesus, would it include clear evidence of a changed life (repentance and intentional service of Jesus) like the woman at the well?

5

The Healing of the Royal Official's Son

A Faith-Building Encounter with Jesus[1]

THROUGH SETTING UP SUCH a striking contrast between the characters of Nicodemus and the Samaritan woman in John 3 and 4, the apostle John invites readers to watch for how other characters will respond to Jesus and his teachings. He also invites readers to watch for other character pairs. He has shown us that some individuals quickly understand and embrace Jesus and his teachings (the Samaritan woman and others from her town), while others struggle with misunderstanding (Nicodemus). So, as we encounter the next two major characters who are paired by healing stories in John's Gospel, one at the end of John 4 and one at the beginning of John 5, we approach these texts with anticipation, waiting to see whether these characters will understand and believe like the Samaritan woman or will miss the point like Nicodemus.

As we come to 4:43–54, Jesus had just left the Samaritan town of Sychar to finish his journey to Galilee (remember 4:3). When he arrived in Galilee, he was welcomed like a hero, because many of the Galileans had been in Jerusalem and witnessed his amazing deeds (4:43–45). The account that follows, however, is not about Jesus' countrymen; it is about "a royal official" from Capernaum whose son was very ill (4:46). Although some

---

1. Although there are many similarities between the healing of the official's son in John 4 and the healing of the centurion's servant in Matt 8:5–13 and Luke 7:1–10, the differences show us that these passages are referring to a different event. More importantly, the placement of this account in the Gospel of John serves to teach distinctive lessons, particularly as this pericope is read against the following healing narrative(s).

have suggested that this official was a Gentile, the Gospel of John does not tell us that. What it tells us is that he was a "royal." The term that John uses likely indicates that he was a relative of the royal Herodian family.[2] For us, that may seem like mere trivia, but for the original readers that description would have painted this man as someone who would not have been held in high regard by the average Jew, because of his connection to the current ruler of Galilee, Herod Antipas.

Antipas, his family, and those who worked for him tended to be viewed as Jews who had compromised their faith and chosen to live like Romans. They were wealthy and were not concerned with living as devout Jews. Antipas, in fact, was known for marrying his brother's wife, Herodias, and then imprisoning John the Baptist after John rebuked him for doing this. And he later killed John the Baptist. This is the ruler whom the official in our passage served and to whom he was likely related. As a result, he would have been viewed in a highly negative way by pious Jews.

Careful readers will notice a pattern emerging. Although we will not attempt to read the account of the royal official against the preceding account of the Samaritan woman in detail, it is important to recognize one aspect of how the contiguous accounts of these two characters convey meaning in the narrative. By presenting them as another character pair, the narrator highlights something important. Just as the despised Samaritan woman encounters Jesus and believes, so also the despised Herodian collaborator encounters Jesus and believes. Taken together, these two accounts serve to drive home the profound truth that readers had encountered in John 3: "For God so loved the world that he gave his only Son, so that *everyone* who believes in him may not perish but may have eternal life" (3:16). No one is excluded from eternal life, if they believe.

In John's account, this royal official had a son who was very ill (4:46). In fact, his son was on the verge of dying (4:49). Although this man was an important official, he urgently hurried from Capernaum to Cana, found Jesus, and then proceeded to beg him to return to Capernaum with him to heal his son. Jesus uses the man's words to accuse the crowd around him of being infatuated with the miraculous signs he was doing and of

---

2. The Greek title βασιλικός (*basilikos*) simply refers to a "royal." This man was most likely related to Herod Antipas and was thus more than a royal employee. Although Antipas, the son of Herod the Great, was not technically a king, he ruled over Galilee and Perea from around 4 BC–AD 39, and he and his family were treated as local royalty. It is possible, though much less likely, that this royal official was a Roman "royal" who had been sent by Caesar.

The Healing of the Royal Official's Son

requiring such signs before they would believe (4:48). The royal official, though, was not deterred by this rebuke. He continued to plead with Jesus to make the trip to Capernaum to heal his son (4:49). And Jesus responded to the man's request, but not in the way he expected. Jesus merely told the man to go home because his son would recover (4:50). And we are surprised to learn—or at least the original readers would have been surprised to learn—that this royal official "believed the word that Jesus spoke to him and started on his way" (4:50).

We then read that "as he was going down, his slaves met him and told him that his child was alive" (4:51). At this point in the story, it is important to keep the geography in mind. The royal official would have left Jesus at about 1:00 p.m. (lit. "the seventh hour," 4:52), but he could not travel the 15 miles back to Capernaum in half a day. So, he would have had to spend the night somewhere along the way. This is why when he finally was met by his servants, he learned that his son's fever had left him the day before, right when Jesus had pronounced him healed (4:52). The account then concludes with these profound words: "The father realized that this was the hour when Jesus had said to him, 'Your son will live.' So he himself believed, along with his whole household" (4:53). As with the Samaritan woman, then, we see another account of a character's interaction with Jesus leading to belief not just for the individual, but for others as well.

Lessons in Discipleship: The Royal Official

There are a number of lessons we can learn about discipleship from the account of the royal official. First, modern readers can easily miss something important in the royal official's actions: "When he heard that Jesus had come from Judea to Galilee, he went and begged him to come down and heal his son, for he was at the point of death" (4:47). It took considerable effort for the royal official to travel to Cana and beg Jesus to intervene on behalf of his son. More than that, it took faith. He had no doubt heard the stories about Jesus' miracles and compassion and when faced with a personal need he chose to believe those stories and to act on his belief. Fifteen miles would have been a significant journey before the age of trains, planes, and automobiles, but this did not deter this man who believed that Jesus could heal his son.[3] This reminds readers that the type of belief that leads to life shows itself in action.

---

3. People would generally not travel more than about 20 miles in a single day, and

The Making of a Disciple

When Jesus responds to the official's request, he groups the royal official with the Jewish crowd surrounding him: "Unless you [plural] see signs and wonders you will not believe" (4:48). Unlike the crowd, though, the royal official already believed. He believed that if Jesus came to Capernaum, his son would be healed (4:49).[4] And Jesus responded to this man's faith by saying, "Go; your son will live" (4:50). Once again, we see the importance of faith. Faith changes everything. Someone can be a despised member of a community, like the Samaritan woman and (likely) the royal official, but when they turn to God in faith, God responds favorably.

Notice also the final expression of the official's faith, because there is an important lesson here: "The man believed the word that Jesus spoke to him and started on his way" (4:50). Again, we see belief leading to appropriate action. The royal official does not question Jesus' pronouncement in any way. He accepts what Jesus says as truth and acts accordingly. When Jesus says something, do we respond like the official did and take immediate action? Do we take him at his word (4:50), even when what he says sounds impossible? This important official humbled himself and publicly asked Jesus for help. Then, when Jesus told him to return home and he would find his son healed, the man did not question him. He believed what Jesus had said and he obeyed.

As we have already seen, the Gospel of John is all about what it means to "believe" in Jesus. In 1:12, we were told, "But to all who received him, who believed in his name, he gave power to become children of God." We quickly learned, though, that not all belief in Jesus leads to someone becoming a child of God: "When he was in Jerusalem during the Passover festival, many believed in his name because they saw the signs that he was doing. But Jesus on his part would not entrust himself to them, because he knew all people and needed no one to testify about anyone; for he himself knew what was in everyone" (2:23–25). In this passage, we see Jesus again seemingly referring to a deficient type of belief that first requires a sign: "Unless you see signs and wonders you will not believe" (4:48). That statement, though, is strikingly contrasted with the faith of the royal official. The official believed before he had seen Jesus work a miracle. As a result, he both sought out Jesus' help in the first place and then responded in absolute

---

that assumed that they started their journey early in the morning; Keener, *Gospel of John*, 1.633.

4. The royal official's faith thus "was confirmed by a sign, not based upon a sign." Koester, *Symbolism in the Fourth Gospel*, 52.

The Healing of the Royal Official's Son

faith when Jesus told him to go home. In fact, we are explicitly told that the man believed before he witnessed the sign that Jesus performed: "Jesus said to him, 'Go; your son will live.' The man believed the word that Jesus spoke to him and started on his way" (4:50). And the final words of this account lead us to conclude that this man and his entire family became children of God because they believed (4:53).

There is something important in 4:53 that is easy to miss, but that continues the same theme we have seen developing thus far in the Gospel of John. We are told not only that the royal official believed, but that he "believed, along with his whole household" (4:53). Why is this detail included? We would suggest its inclusion naturally leads readers to fill in a gap in the narrative. In the chronology of 4:50–53, the royal official leaves Cana and, as he is returning home, he is met by his servants who tell him that his son recovered at precisely the time Jesus announced he would live. The next thing we read is: "The father realized that this was the hour when Jesus had said to him, 'Your son will live.' So he himself believed, along with his whole household" (4:53). We are not surprised that the father put two and two together and believed. But how did his whole household believe? His whole household had not made the journey to meet him. They had merely sent some of his slaves for that task (4:51). The narrator leaves the reader to infer that the royal official told his whole household what had happened so that they too would believe. Thus, once again, we see a picture of someone encountering Jesus, coming to believe, and then pointing others to the Messiah by telling them what he had done. While the latter point is not emphasized in this passage, the surprising words, "along with his whole household," lead us to naturally infer that information, particularly when we have already come to expect that pattern.

Finally, notice the royal official's journey *from* faith *to* faith. Remember that one of the primary ways we discover meaning in narratives is through identifying the main characters, and then considering how their actions lead to particular consequences. When the royal official's son becomes seriously ill, he acts on the faith that he already has (Jesus is able to heal) and makes the trip to seek help from Jesus. The faith that he demonstrates is not yet the type of faith that leads to life (1:12; 3:16), but it is the type of faith that leads to a favorable response from Jesus. The first consequence, then, of acting on his limited faith is the healing of his son. But the consequences do not end there. For, we see at the end of the passage that the royal official now "himself believed" (4:53). We might quickly say, "He had already believed!" That conclusion, however, would miss the point that is being made in the Gospel of John. There is belief and there is *belief*. There is belief that saves and there is belief that does not save. And in this case, as the royal official experienced Jesus' response to his limited belief, that belief matured into saving faith in Jesus the Messiah. The pattern that we see here thus illustrates what we read elsewhere in the words of Jesus when he told his disciples, "Then pay attention to how you listen; for to those who have, more will be given; and from those who do not have, even what they seem to have will be taken away" (Luke 8:18). This saying of Jesus, which occurs in more than one context in the Synoptic Gospels, likely points to the fact that those who exercise the faith they have will experience more faith.[5]

Lessons in Discipleship: Jesus

In addition to the lessons in discipleship that we learn from the actions of the royal official and the consequences of those actions, two things stand out in this passage as we consider what Jesus' actions teach us about discipleship. First, Jesus' response to the royal official, "Unless you see signs and wonders you will not believe" (4:48), is surprising until we place it in its larger narrative context. At first glance, Jesus seems to rebuke a frantic parent who humbly comes to him for help. The "you," though, is plural. We should likely understand Jesus' words, then, as Jesus taking the opportunity to confront the crowd that had gathered with their failure to believe in him. In other words, Jesus is confronting unbelief. He does not gloss over it, nor does he pander to the crowd's fickle desires for a supernatural show. He calls them out for their failure to believe in him. And this, too, is a responsibility of those who claim to be Jesus' disciples. His disciples are called to point others to Jesus, but they are not called to ignore stubborn unbelief when it confronts them. Like Jesus, as they present others with the amazing things he has done, not least of which his coming to earth to die for their sins, they should not hesitate to confront them with the foolishness of choosing to reject Jesus and the life he offers to all who "believe."

Second, and related, we see that Jesus calls people to move beyond infatuation with miracles to genuine belief in him. We see this both in his rebuke of the crowd (4:48) and in his challenge to the royal official to take him at his word (4:50). Jesus could have gone to Capernaum with the royal official and healed his son. Instead, he invited the royal official to move

---

5. Paul may be making a similar point in Phil 3:16, though this is disputed.

The Healing of the Royal Official's Son

from a sight-based "faith" to saving faith by believing his word before he saw the miracle. He invited him to choose to live by faith, rather than by sight.

Jesus was and is a worker of miracles, but faith that depends on miracles is not the type of faith that Jesus calls people to in the Gospel of John. Those whose "faith" rests on miracles, rather than on the Word of God, easily fall away when they do not experience the miracles they are looking for at particular points in their life. Many disciples today need to hear Jesus' rebuke of those who demand signs. When disciples demand that God intervene in miraculous (or even particular) ways in their lives, they often miss out on God's purposes for them.

Finally, we are told at the end of the passage that "this was the second sign Jesus did after coming from Judea to Galilee" (4:54). Jesus' first "sign"[6] (2:10) led his disciples to believe in him (2:11). His talk with the Samaritan woman at the well led her and many of the people of Sychar to believe in him (4:1–42). Now, Jesus' second "sign" in Galilee leads a man and his whole household to believe in him. Taken together, Jesus' actions in the first chapters of the Gospel of John make it clear that he is eager to reveal himself to people because he is eager for people to believe and receive eternal life. And his eagerness to do so should spur every disciple to be eager to make Jesus known to others.

---

6. Because John refers to the healing of the official's son as Jesus' "second sign," scholars have traditionally spoken of seven signs that Jesus performs in the Gospel of John (2:1–11; 4:46–54; 5:1–15; 6:5–14; 6:16–24; 9:1–7; 11:1–45). In reality, we are told that this was "the second sign that Jesus did *when he had come from Judea to Galilee*" (4:54). We already know from 2:23 that Jesus had done many other signs *in Jerusalem*: "When he was in Jerusalem during the Passover festival, many believed in his name because they saw the signs that he was doing." (2:23; see also 4:45). Nicodemus also referred to more than one sign that Jesus had done prior to their conversation (3:2). And Jesus' knowledge of the Samaritan woman's sinful past relationships should also be viewed as a sign, especially since it led people to believe in him. What John refers to here, then, was Jesus' second sign *in Galilee*. It might be surprising to readers that John does not include all of the signs that Jesus performed, but later he writes that Jesus did many other signs that he did not incorporate into his gospel (20:30; see also 21:25).

Questions for Disciples

1. What kind of faith in Jesus do you have? Is it a faith that demands miracles or a faith that is quick to act on whatever he says?

2. Has your faith grown as you have acted on what God has revealed to you? Or has it perhaps remained immature because of failure to believe what Jesus has said and act on it?

3. Do you expect Jesus to respond to your faith by asking you to exercise more faith, as he did with the royal official?

4. Has your household heard what Jesus has done for them through your witness?

5. Do you have friends or family members whose "faith" demands miracles? How might you gently or firmly urge them to take Jesus at his word?

6. Are you infatuated with miracles or infatuated with Jesus?

6

The Healing of the Sick Man at the Pool
A Selfish Encounter with Jesus

THE HEALING OF THE royal official's son at the end of John 4 is the first healing in the Gospel of John. And it is a healing that leads to belief. As we move into John 5, then, where we encounter Jesus interacting with another individual in need of healing, we not only recognize a character pairing, but we naturally expect a similar outcome. What we discover instead is a character who stands in sharp contrast to the royal official.

In John 5:1–15, we find the story of a man who had been lame for thirty-eight years whom Jesus encounters at a pool where many sick and lame people gathered, hoping to be healed. These desperate individuals embraced what appears to have been a Jewish superstition that an angel would occasionally cause the waters of the pool at Bethesda to move, indicating that God's power was available for healing.[1] We are not told what the man's specific ailment was. We are only told that he "had been ill for thirty-eight years" (5:5). The fact that he spent his time among a group of people who were "blind, lame, and paralyzed" (5:3) makes it clear that he was *seriously* ill. The fact that he had been in this state for thirty-eight years tells us that he was also *chronically* ill. The fact that he needed someone to move him

---

1. An important textual variant is found in 5:3b–4, where some later biblical witnesses add, wholly or in part, "waiting for the stirring of the waters for an angel of the Lord went down at certain seasons into the pool, and stirred up the water; whoever stepped in first after the stirring of the water was made well from whatever disease that person had." The earliest and most reliable witnesses do not contain this comment. This addition to the text seems to have been inserted later by a scribe who was trying to explain why the man answered Jesus the way he did in 5:7. See Metzger, *Textual Commentary*, 179.

(5:7) tells us that his illness had likely left him bedridden and requiring assistance in order to move about. Now, we are prepared to see how Jesus engages this man in conversation, how this man responds, and what their interactions teach us about discipleship.

Jesus intentionally chooses to approach this particular man, but he does not simply pronounce him healed. Once again, he asks a question that is designed to start a conversation. It is a question that might surprise us: "Do you want to be made well?" (5:6). Of course, he wants to be made well! Jesus, however, is not a quick-fix miracle worker. And his question in 5:6 is going to work with his later statements to the man after he has been healed to communicate something important, "See, you have been made well! Do not sin any more, so that nothing worse happens to you" (5:14). Read together with the question in 5:6, Jesus' words in 5:14 imply another question: "Do you want to *stay* well?" We'll come back to this issue below.

We might have expected the man to simply respond, "Yes, I want to be made well! Will you please heal me?" But this man appears to have no knowledge of Jesus or his ability to heal. So, like Nicodemus, he responds to Jesus—the one who was with God and was God (1:1)—from an earthly perspective: "The sick man answered him, 'Sir, I have no one to put me into the pool when the water is stirred up; and while I am making my way, someone else steps down ahead of me'" (5:7). Whatever we make of his belief that the pool periodically had healing properties, the man was still relying on conventional wisdom, even though he was standing in the presence of the one through whom all things were created (1:3). He despaired over his predicament, rather than looking with hope to the omnipotent Word of God who could easily help him in his difficult circumstances. He had set his hope on the stirred waters of a pool, not realizing that the one who offers living water (4:10) that leads to eternal life (4:14) was standing before him. Despite his failure to look to Jesus for help, however, Jesus chose to intervene anyway: "Stand up, take your mat and walk" (5:8). And we are not surprised to read the result of Jesus' words: "At once, the man was made well, and he took up his mat and began to walk" (5:9).

The story, however, is not yet over. We are left wondering, "How will this man respond to the amazing thing that Jesus has done for him?" Will he show no response, like Nicodemus? Or, will he run off to tell others about what Jesus has done for him, like the Samaritan woman?

At this point, the narrative turns our attention to a familiar character group in the Gospel of John, "the Jews." This phrase is often a short way

The Healing of the Sick Man at the Pool

of referring to "the Jewish leaders," as here, but is sometimes used more broadly to refer to Jesus' own people who did not embrace him (1:11). One of the reasons the Jewish leaders did not embrace Jesus was because of theological disagreements they had with him. They had, for example, a robust theology of the Sabbath, which comes into play in this passage and at many other points during Jesus' ministry years. God had instructed his people to treat the Sabbath day differently than every other day:

> Remember the sabbath day, and keep it holy. Six days you shall labor and do all your work. But the seventh day is a sabbath to the Lord your God; you shall not do any work—you, your son or your daughter, your male or female slave, your livestock, or the alien resident in your towns. For in six days the Lord made heaven and earth, the sea, and all that is in them, but rested the seventh day; therefore the Lord blessed the sabbath day and consecrated it. (Exod 20:8–11)

Keeping the Sabbath was one of the Ten Commandments and thus a command that must be taken very seriously. No work was to be done on the Sabbath. Over the centuries, particularly in the last two centuries prior to Jesus coming to earth, Jewish leaders (Pharisees) had put significant effort into spelling out everything that qualified as "work" that must be avoided on the Sabbath. And their decisions on these matters came to carry as much weight and authority as Scripture itself. Since it was a Sabbath day (5:9b) and the Jews saw the man carrying his mat, they quickly pounced on him: "It is the sabbath; it is not lawful for you to carry your mat" (5:10). Now, there is nowhere in the Old Testament where God said, "Thou shall not carry a mat on the sabbath," but the Jewish leaders had broadened the definition of "labor" and "work" from Exod 20:9 to include almost any type of activity that would involve doing something other than sitting, sleeping, worshiping, eating, or going to the toilet.[2] So, they confronted the poor healed man as a lawbreaker.

Notice a detail in the story that we might easily rush past: "So the Jews said to *the man who had been cured*" (5:10). Why is this detail important? We have just seen Jesus do an amazing miracle. Although we are not told that the Jewish leaders witnessed the miracle, we are reminded that they

---

2. Oral law of the Pharisees, later transcribed in the Mishnah (ca. second century AD), lists thirty-nine activities that the Pharisees considered forbidden on a Sabbath. Interestingly, carrying one's mat (moving an object from one place to another) was one of the prohibited acts (*m. Šabb* 7.2).

are confronting a man who had just been cured of an illness that had been ongoing for thirty-eight years, and it is implied that they were aware of this miracle. The response that the apostle John records from them, then, should shock us. How could they not give glory to God for this amazing miracle? How could they fail to rejoice with this poor man who had suffered so much, but had now been healed? How could they not want to meet Jesus themselves and sit as his feet? Instead, their man-made theology leads them to miss the point. And unlike the Samaritan woman who was able to get past the theological question of where God should be worshiped, this character group never gets it. They are more committed to their theology than they are to God.

Their surprising response leads us as readers to wonder how the healed man will respond to Jesus. When Jesus commanded him to stand up, pick up his mat, and walk, the man discovered that he had been "made well, and took up his mat and began to walk" (5:9). His astounding healing, however, did not lead him to believe in Jesus or seek to tell others about what Jesus had done. Why? The narrator tells us that the healed man did not know who Jesus was because Jesus had quickly "disappeared in the crowd that was there" (5:13). This leads us to wonder what will happen when this man connects his healing to Jesus. Will he then believe?

Notice what happens next in the story. Jesus once again takes the initiative to interact with this man. Jesus went and "found him in the temple" (5:14). We might have expected Jesus to invite this man to be "born from above" (3:3) or to drink "living water" from him (4:10), but this time Jesus says something very different: "See, you have been made well! Do not sin any more, so that nothing worse happens to you" (5:14). Jesus has brought physical healing to this man, but he is not content to leave the man physically healed without also addressing the man's spiritual health. He essentially invites the man to believe in him by submitting to his command to repent and by changing his view of sin.

Modern readers are often quick to condemn the Pharisees for their emphasis on rules, but this passage and the rest of the Bible reminds us that rules are not the problem. The problem was that the Pharisees had replaced the Word of God with their own traditions. This was a great offense to God and it is why Jesus soundly rebukes them elsewhere: "You have a fine way of rejecting the commandment of God in order to keep your tradition!" (Mark 7:9). Human religious traditions are oppressive and they undermine the authority of God's Word, but rightly rejecting those traditions should

The Healing of the Sick Man at the Pool

not lead disciples of Jesus to reject the commands found in God's Word as if they too were oppressive. God's Word specifically and consistently reminds us that God expects obedience to his commands and those commands are not oppressive: "For the love of God is this, that we obey his commandments. And his commandments are not burdensome" (1 John 5:3). This is why Jesus can, on the one hand, reject the religious traditions of the Jewish leaders, while at the same time insisting on obedience to God's commands: "Do not sin any more, so that nothing worse happens to you" (John 5:14).

How did the healed man respond to Jesus' command? On the one hand, as in the case of Nicodemus, the response appears to be noncommittal. Remember, though, that the gospel writers deliberately selected what to include in their accounts of the life and teachings of Jesus in order to teach readers particular lessons. Here, we expect the man to respond to Jesus' words with deep gratitude for his healing, with belief in Jesus because of his powerful miracle, and with a commitment to living in obedience to God's commands, given Jesus' strong exhortation. Instead, we see something very different. The Jewish leaders had asked the man who had healed him. Once Jesus makes the effort to reveal himself to the man as the one who had healed him, rather than being eager to follow Jesus, the man is eager to report Jesus to the authorities! "The man went away and told the Jews that it was Jesus who had made him well" (5:15). How can this be? We can understand how the man was eager to protect himself from unwanted consequences from the Jewish leaders by telling them that by carrying his mat he was simply doing what the person who had healed him had instructed (5:11). His response in 5:15, though, suggests that he "would have been quite willing to turn Jesus in to save himself from prosecution as a Sabbath breaker"[3] even at that point. The result of the healed man's actions was predictable: "Therefore the Jews started persecuting Jesus, because he was doing such things on the sabbath" (5:16). Surely, this man, who had himself experienced the wrath of the Jewish leaders for carrying his mat, knew that they would persecute Jesus if he identified him as the "culprit." But he did it anyway. As Michaels points out,

> there was no reason why he had to do this. He himself was in the clear so far as the charge of Sabbath breaking was concerned. He had told the authorities he did not know who had told him to pick up his mat, and that could have ended it. Yet now, having met Jesus in the temple, he suddenly becomes very scrupulous about the

---

3. Michaels, "Invalid at the Pool," 341.

unfinished business, returning to volunteer information he had been unable to supply before . . . and he becomes in the end an informant.[4]

Instead of belief, instead of "receiving" Jesus (1:12), the healed man acts against the one who had healed him. The man's betrayal, in fact, leads to the most heated persecution of Jesus up to this point in the Gospel of John. The conflict that follows finds Jesus revealing that both he and the Father work on the Sabbath (5:17), confirming the religious leaders' fears that Jesus was not only publicly rejecting their traditions but was also "making himself equal to God" (5:18). This leads them to actively pursue Jesus' death. So, in the end, the character of the healed man in John 5 represents a person who, after encountering Jesus in a profound way, not only fails to become his disciple, but also actively and selfishly opposes him.[5] Jesus seeks out the healed man to reveal his identity to him (a gracious act) and the healed man seeks out the authorities to reveal Jesus' identity to them (a wicked act). What are we to make of all of this? What does this account of the character of the healed man in John 5 teach us about discipleship?

Lessons in Discipleship: The Sick Man in John 5

Like Nicodemus in John 3, we find no indication that the man who was healed in John 5 became a disciple of Jesus at this point. Nevertheless, he presents us with some valuable lessons about discipleship. Remember, meaning in narratives is communicated, to a significant degree, through the actions of the main characters and the consequences of those actions. In the case of the healed man in John 5, we learn three closely related lessons.

First, we learn that to become a disciple of Jesus requires that we set aside our own selfish desires and embrace what Jesus desires for us. In John 5, we encounter a character who has a genuine need, but who shows no interest in the one who healed him, other than to make problems for him. He is a selfish man who cares only for himself. And his selfishness leads him to be content with physical healing—which lasts until death, at best—when he could have received so much more from Jesus: eternal life. Disciples of Jesus recognize how inferior physical healing is to the abundant and eternal life that God offers. They also recognize that those who are only interested

---

4. Michaels, "Invalid at the Pool," 344–45.
5. Culpepper adds that the man "represents those whom even the signs cannot lead to authentic faith." Culpepper, *Anatomy*, 138.

The Healing of the Sick Man at the Pool

in God for what God can do for them will never have the kind of faith that brings eternal life.

Second, when we read of a man who had suffered horribly for thirty-eight years being healed by Jesus, we are shocked that he shows no gratitude for what God had done for him. This lack of gratitude is likely connected to his wicked act of turning Jesus in to the authorities. In Romans 1, we read about the fundamental sin of which most of the human race is guilty: "they did not honor him as God or give thanks to him" (Rom 1:21). When God acts on our behalf, it is critical that disciples give him the glory and thanksgiving that is due him. Notice what happens to those who fail to do that: "they became futile in their thinking, and their senseless minds were darkened" (Rom 1:21). When we fail to give God thanks for what he has done for us, we run the risk of allowing our selfishness to utterly distort our thinking so that we act just as foolishly as the man who was healed in John 5. Failure to express gratitude to God is dangerous. Genuine disciples of Jesus live with a profound sense of gratitude to God for what he has done for them.

Third, the healed man was content with his situation after he had been healed. He had been sick; now he was healed. And that seems to be all that mattered to him. Disciples of Jesus, on the other hand, live with a holy discontentment. Paul describes this holy discontentment in Phil 3:

> Yet whatever gains I had, these I have come to regard as loss because of Christ. More than that, I regard everything as loss because of the surpassing value of knowing Christ Jesus my Lord. For his sake I have suffered the loss of all things, and I regard them as rubbish, in order that I may gain Christ and be found in him, not having a righteousness of my own that comes from the law, but one that comes through faith in Christ, the righteousness from God based on faith. I want to know Christ and the power of his resurrection and the sharing of his sufferings by becoming like him in his death, if somehow I may attain the resurrection from the dead. (Phil 3:7–11)

Did Paul already know Christ Jesus? Of course! He had not only met him on the road to Damascus (Acts 9) and been taken up to heaven and had amazing things revealed to him (2 Cor 12), but he had also experienced the presence and power of Jesus in his life for many years. Even so, we read in this passage of Paul's eager longing to know Christ far more deeply. This is precisely what the healed man in John 5 lacked. He appears to have had no desire to know Jesus at all. He only wanted a better life for himself. And his attitude toward Jesus encourages us as readers to examine our own attitude toward Jesus.

Lessons in Discipleship: Jesus in John 5

In addition to the discipleship lessons that we learn from the selfish healed man in John 5, we also learn important lessons about discipleship from Jesus himself. First, Jesus models for us the importance of helping those to whom we minister, believers or unbelievers, to own their dire need before we show them how God can meet that need. Acknowledging need is a critical prerequisite for someone becoming a follower of Jesus. It is also a critical starting point for spiritual growth in those who are already disciples of Jesus. Those who think they have already arrived, condemn themselves to never actually getting to where they need to go. Jesus' question, "Do you want to be made well?" should ring in the ears of not only unbelievers, but believers as well. For, the more believers grow in their faith, the more God reveals areas of their life where they remain unwell and still need to be healed.

Second, we see from Jesus' actions that discipleship can never be divorced from turning from sin. Jesus invites people to "come just as they are" to him for salvation, but he never invites anyone to remain just as they are. In fact, even "coming just as you are" can easily be distorted into thinking one need not repent of sin in order to receive the gift of eternal life. Disciples must resist the lie that followers of Jesus are not called to live holy lives. Saving belief in Jesus requires turning from sin.

Third, Jesus' words to the healed man remind us that sin can have major consequences in life. During Jesus' day, many Jews believed that all sickness was the consequence of sin. This is precisely what we will see in the next chapter as Jesus' disciples consider why a man had been born blind (9:1–2) and Jesus corrects the view that suffering is always caused by sin (9:3). Here, on the other hand, Jesus seems to affirm, in this particular case, that a connection does exist between the man's sin and his suffering. Moreover, Jesus warns the man that if he went back to his sinful ways, he could expect suffering once again: "Do not sin any more, so that nothing worse happens to you" (John 5:14). This should not surprise us since the New Testament depicts that some specific calamities may be the consequence of specific sin (e.g., 1 Cor 11:30). Yet, by far the biggest danger facing this man is not physical infirmity, but dying in his sin without coming to a saving faith in the Messiah (John 8:24). So, as we look at this episode at the pool of Bethesda, considering both Jesus' teaching and the actions of the sick man and consequences of those actions, we cannot avoid the fact that part of the lesson for disciples here is that there are practical consequences of sin. That is just one of the reasons disciples should be eager to avoid sin.

Finally, disciples dare not miss the fact that Jesus refuses to give the teachings of men the same authority as the Word of God. And neither should we. To follow Jesus' example as his disciples, though, we must first know the Word of God well enough to recognize when someone is promoting the traditions of men, rather than the authoritative teachings of God. Had Jesus followed the traditions of men in this passage, he would not have acted to bring about the sick man's healing. In the same way, when disciples of Jesus are bound by the traditions of men, their ability to serve God will often be significantly undermined.

Questions for Disciples

1. Do you view your physical needs as more important than your spiritual needs?
2. Do you try to get things from Jesus and then get on with your life? Does your relationship with Christ revolve around what you can get from him?
3. Are there times when you have failed to show gratitude to God for what he has done for you?
4. Are you content with a superficial relationship with Jesus or do you have a "holy discontentment" that spurs you to go deeper?
5. Have you recognized that being a disciple of Jesus necessarily involves forsaking sin?
6. Are there parts of your belief system that are merely human teachings rather than coming from the Word of God?

7

The Healing of the Blind Man
A Life-Changing Encounter with Jesus

As we move on from the story of the man healed at the pool of Bethesda in John 5, we read a lot about Jesus' teachings and ministry in John 6–8. We might assume that the apostle John is finished recording healing stories. After all, he had already given us a character pair with the royal official and the man at the pool. And we do not encounter another major character until John 9. As it turns out, though, this character, like the last major character, also needs healing.

Although the accounts of the man at the pool in John 5 and the man born blind in John 9 are separated by a lot of teaching, they are linked by the fact that both involve the healing of an individual who had been suffering for a very long time, both take place on the Sabbath, and both lead to controversies over Jesus' right to heal on the Sabbath. These details, and the fact that the man born blind is the next major character to appear in the narrative, help us to see that the apostle John has added an additional character to the character pairing of the royal official and the man at the pool, giving us three healing stories, rather than two, to read together.

The story of the healing of the man born blind in John 9 provides us with a response to Jesus that differs dramatically from what we saw in John 5, but that has similarities to the healing account in John 4. This time, we encounter a character who is not only miraculously healed physically, but who is also transformed spiritually. The one who has just revealed himself to be "the light of the world" (8:12; 9:5) miraculously floods with light the life of a man who had previously lived his whole life in darkness! And the

The Healing of the Blind Man

way that Jesus does this helps us to understand some important features of what it looks like to become his disciple.

The account of the blind man's healing in 9:1-12 has several interesting components. First, in contrast to the last healing story in John 5, here we learn that this man's sickness is not the result of sin, contrary to the disciples' working assumption. As we pointed out above, some rabbis of the day believed that all sickness was the consequence of personal sin, so they were forced to come up with theories about why some children were born blind or lame or deaf. Some suggested that it was the result of their parents' sin, while others maintained that the child had actually sinned in the womb and thus paid the price by being born unwell! Jesus makes it clear that this man's blindness from birth had nothing to do with sin.

Next, when Jesus approaches the man, he does something very strange: "he spat on the ground and made mud with the saliva and spread the mud on the man's eyes" (9:6). Why would Jesus do such a strange thing? It does not sound very hygienic! The key is found in Jesus' next actions. He told the blind man, "Go, wash in the pool of Siloam" (9:7). And to make the key point clearer, John informs his readers that "Siloam" means "sent." The One who was sent into the world by the Father to save the world (3:17) sends this blind man to a pool to wash as the first step in his salvation.

What must the blind man do in order to be healed? He must believe Jesus. And that belief will be expressed by obeying Jesus. He could have said, "How ridiculous! A man makes mud from his own spit, smears it on the eyes of a blind man, and then tells that blind man to make his way to the pool of Siloam and wash the nasty stuff off his eyes there!" But that is not what the blind man did. Instead, he obeyed Jesus and came back able to see (9:7). In the next few verses, the man's neighbors come on the scene to question him about the healing. And the healed man takes this opportunity to testify about his encounter with Jesus (9:8-12). Notice that, unlike the man who was healed in John 5, the blind man knows who had healed him and is eager to give credit to Jesus. In fact, throughout this account we see a very different attitude toward Jesus, the one who had healed him, than we saw in John 5.

Look at the next part of the story in 9:13-34. The healing of the blind man should have been cause for great celebration among the Jewish people and the Jewish leaders. Instead, the healed blind man was immediately confronted by the Pharisees who questioned the authenticity of his healing. A little note in the text warns us of what is to come: "Now it was a sabbath day when Jesus made the mud and opened his eyes" (9:14). We already saw the backlash that healing on a Sabbath day had brought from the Jewish leaders in John 5. When the Pharisees ask the man how he had been healed, for the second time we hear the man testify about Jesus, this time in a very matter of fact manner: "He put mud on my eyes. Then I washed, and now I see" (9:15). It was that simple! "Jesus said to do something; I obeyed Jesus; and now I am healed," he tells them.

We are quite astonished that the Pharisees do not give glory to God for this great miracle. Instead, they go back to their own traditions. Nowhere in Scripture does it say that spitting on the ground, or rubbing mud on someone's eyes, or healing someone would break the command to keep the Sabbath day holy. But according to the Pharisees' own traditions, such actions were not allowed.[1] So, some of them accused Jesus of breaking the Sabbath and insisted that such actions proved that he was "not from God" (9:16). Their words contrast with the earlier words of Nicodemus, "no one can do these signs that you do apart from the presence of God" (3:2). Not all of the Pharisees were so blind, though. Others wondered how Jesus could perform such signs, if he were a sinner (9:16). So they pressed the formerly blind man about what he believed concerning the one who had healed him, and the healed man exclaimed that Jesus must be a prophet (9:17).

The man's proclamation about Jesus is met with disbelief by the religious leaders and this leads to a second interrogation. This time, they interrogate the healed man's parents, who confirm that the man was their son and that he had been born blind. They made it clear, though, that they had no idea how their son had been healed. They also insisted that since their son was an adult, he should be the one they questioned instead of them (9:20–23). Notice the reason the parents responded this way: the Jewish authorities "had already agreed that anyone who confessed Jesus to be the Messiah would be put out of the synagogue" (9:22).[2] In yet another example

---

1. As with the healing in John 5, this controversy revolves around Jesus healing on the Sabbath. Yet, in this healing story, Jesus spits on the ground and supposedly becomes guilty of "kneading" by mixing the spit and dirt to make mud. Kneading was one of the thirty-nine activities that the Pharisees asserted as prohibited on a Sabbath (*m. Šabb* 7.2). Once again, the Sabbath controversy was not based on Scripture itself, but rather on rabbinic tradition. In addition to the making of the mud itself, it is likely that the Pharisees would see the application of the mud and the washing off of the mud as further evidence of breaking the Sabbath. Moreover, as with the healing on the Sabbath in John 5, one gets the impression that Jesus was happy to break the oral traditions of the Pharisees to create an opportunity to reveal what really matters to God.

2. Schürer notes that this act would have been the harshest banishment from the

The Healing of the Blind Man

of character contrast, their fear of being banned from the synagogue stands in sharp contrast to the courage of their son who boldly acknowledges what Jesus had done for him.[3]

Following this interaction, the religious leaders summoned the healed man for another interrogation (9:24–34). In this scene, the formerly blind man makes further statements that reveal the progression of his budding faith. First, when the Pharisees essentially tell him to be honest because they know that Jesus is a sinner, the healed man makes one of the most profound statements in the entire Bible: "I do not know whether he is a sinner. One thing I do know, that though I was blind, now I see" (9:25). The Pharisees' thinking was bound by the theological box in which they insisted everything must fit. They assumed that anything that did not match their traditions must be wrong. The formerly blind man, on the other hand, pointed to the undeniable fact that his life has been dramatically changed by the one whom they are calling a sinner. And then, when they continued to question him about how he had been healed, he asked them whether they also wanted to become Jesus' disciples (9:27). His question to them is both the action of a disciple (pointing others to Jesus) and implies by the language he uses ("Do you *also* want to become his disciples?") that he already considered himself to be Jesus' disciple (9:27). Then, in 9:33, as the Pharisees refuse to acknowledge where Jesus "comes from," the man proclaims that Jesus must be "from God" or he could not have healed him (9:33). This apparently simple man's confident knowledge and bold witness was based on his encounter with Jesus (9:30–33) and led him to stand firm against what the Pharisees thought they knew about how God works (9:29).[4] In fact, the formerly blind man, who had a brand new relationship with Jesus, showed remarkable theological insight:

> The man answered, "Here is an astonishing thing! You do not know where he comes from, and yet he opened my eyes. We know that God does not listen to sinners, but he does listen to one who worships him and obeys his will. Never since the world began has it been heard that anyone opened the eyes of a person born

---

synagogue, a permanent excommunication of the offender. Schürer, *History of the Jewish People*, 2:59–62. See also John 12:42 and 16:2 for other references to the practice and the fear created by it. For further discussion of how this concept may parallel the persecution of the future Johannine community, see Brown, *Gospel According to John*, 374, 380.

3. See Reimer, "Man Born Blind," 435.
4. See Bennema, *Encountering Jesus*, 252.

blind. If this man were not from God, he could do nothing." (John 9:30–33)

The man's theological arguments are irrefutable, but it comes as no surprise that the Jewish leaders did not appreciate being instructed by someone who did not have the benefit of their theological education. Unable to respond with any argument from Scripture, they essentially resorted to name calling ("You were born entirely in sins," 9:34), reflecting the same wrong understanding of sickness that we saw the disciples had at the beginning of this passage (9:2). They do more, though, than mock the healed man; they also drive him out (9:34), implying that he will no longer be welcome among God's people in the synagogue (9:22). That appears to be the end of the story, but Jesus is not finished with the man he healed of blindness.

In 9:35–41, we learn that after the man had been excommunicated from the synagogue, Jesus found him and asked him, "Do you believe in the Son of Man?" (9:35).[5] When the formerly blind man responded with eagerness to know who this Son of Man was (9:36), Jesus graciously revealed himself to him: "You have seen him, and the one speaking with you is he" (9:37). Notice the incredible revelation that Jesus offers to this man. He informs this man, who had never seen anything in his entire life before that day, that he was *seeing* the "Son of Man" (9:37) standing right in front of him. This direct revelation of his identity resembles Jesus' words to the Samaritan woman after she had mentioned the coming Christ: "I am he, the one who is speaking to you" (4:26).

We had earlier read the profound words that the healed man spoke to the Jewish leaders: "One thing I do know, that though I was blind, now I see" (9:25). Jesus' revelation to the man at the end of this story brings fuller meaning to this statement. Now, the formerly blind man is given the privilege by Jesus of seeing not only with his physical eyes, but also with his spiritual eyes. He now has fullness of sight and is prepared to live as Jesus' disciple. The story thus begins with him receiving physical sight and concludes with him receiving spiritual sight, which is evident in the man's confession of faith ("Lord, I believe") and his worship of Jesus (9:38).

---

5. Jesus may use the title "Son of Man" here as a reference to the Jewish expectation of the heavenly Son of Man who would establish God's kingdom upon the earth after bringing judgment upon unbelievers (compare Dan 7:13–14 with Matt 24:27//Mark 13:26–27//Luke 21:27–28). As John 9:39–41 indicates, judgment is about to be pronounced upon the Pharisees.

The Healing of the Blind Man

The story, though, does not end with the formerly blind man's confession of faith. Our questions regarding how the central character of this story would respond to Jesus have been resolved, but he is not the only major character. The Jewish leaders, who have stubbornly refused to believe, have also been an important character group in this story. And Jesus interacts with them for the first time at the end of John 9. As he had spoken with the healed man, others had been present and were listening. After the healed man believes and worships the Lord, Jesus tells those gathered there, "I came into this world for judgment so that those who do not see may see, and those who do see may become blind" (9:39). While the man has received the light, both on a physical and spiritual level, the religious leaders, who thought themselves to be spiritually discerning and insightful, were in reality proven to be spiritually blinded by their rejection of Jesus (9:39–41).[6] Thus, the man's physical healing becomes a symbol for his spiritual healing, which is contrasted with the spiritual blindness of the religious leaders who choose to remain in darkness.

Reading in Stereo: Three Characters, Three Healings

To fully understand the message of John 9, we need to read it as a companion story to the earlier healing account in John 5. There are many similarities between the two episodes, which serve to link the stories together. (1) Both men had been ill for a very long time. (2) In both accounts, Jesus takes the initiative to heal. (3) Both stories mention a pool of water. (4) In both stories, the healing takes place on the Sabbath. (5) Both individuals are accused of breaking the Sabbath by Jewish leaders. (6) Both individuals are

---

6. John 9:41 uses a second-class conditional clause, or "contrary-to-fact condition," in which the premise is presumed to be untrue for the sake of argument: "If you were blind, you would not have sin." "As in the preceding riddle, the first part revisits in straightforward fashion the story of the man born blind, where he who was literally blind did not 'have sin' [9:3] . . . In asking, 'Are we blind too?' (v. 40), they had implied that of course they were not, and Jesus calls them on it . . . In doing so, he abruptly changes the subject from literal blindness and sight respectively to what has been his preoccupation all along: their response, or lack of it, to himself and to his word." Michaels, *Gospel of John*, 575. "The Pharisees in John 9 think they are sighted and therefore need no healing, when, in fact, the opposite is the case." Pate, *Writings of John*, 117n10. The Pharisees' "journey from sight to blindness is as profound as the man's journey from blindness to sight." Reimer, "Man Born Blind," 436–37.

interrogated by the religious authorities to discover who had healed them. (7) Jesus finds both men later and provides them with further revelation.[7]

Despite the many similarities between the stories, however, the responses of the two healed men to Jesus are markedly different. While the newly healed man in John 9 defends Jesus before the religious authorities, leading to his own excommunication from the synagogue, the newly healed man in John 5 betrays him to the religious authorities. Nowhere in the story in John 5 do we see any expression of gratitude from the healed man toward Jesus.[8] Instead, this man seems to disregard Jesus, turn his back on him, and remain in unbelief. The reaction of the formerly blind man to Jesus could not be more different. He begins with a very limited understanding of who Jesus is (9:11), but when he too is charged with violating the Sabbath (9:16), he defends Jesus, rather than defending himself. And we see him progress in discipleship as the story develops. After being healed by Jesus, he recognizes that Jesus must be a prophet (9:17) who has come from God (9:33). His question to the religious leaders in 9:27 ("Do you *also* want to become his disciples?") likely implies that he already considered himself to be a disciple of Jesus, even though he knew that the religious authorities were clearly opposed to Jesus and anyone who associated with him. Ultimately, this man who had lived his life in darkness recognized that Jesus was the Lord and he worshiped him (9:38).

Why did the apostle John include these two stories in his gospel and present them to us as a character pair? Part of the answer to that question is found in recognizing that the narrative actually presents us with a character *group*. And that group consists of two positive responses to Jesus' healing (John 4 and John 9) that surround a negative response (John 5). The emphasis that the first and third accounts place on saving belief, while at the same time acknowledging the possibility of ongoing unbelief despite an obvious miracle, supports a key feature of the message of the narrative thus far. Throughout the first half of the Gospel of John, we see a range of responses to the signs that Jesus performed. Some are curious like Nicodemus (John 3). Some believe in Jesus' name, like the crowds at the end of John 2, but their belief is a selfish belief that embraces Jesus for what they can get from him (2:23–25). Others, like the Samaritan woman, embrace Jesus on his terms and have their lives transformed.

---

7. For more on the implicit comparisons and contrasts, see Culpepper, *Anatomy*, 139–40.

8. Köstenberger, *John*, 183.

The Healing of the Blind Man

In the three healing accounts of John 4, John 5, and John 9 we see a similar pattern. And by placing the shockingly apathetic response of the healed man in John 5 between the appropriate responses of the royal official and blind man in John 4 and John 9, we see the profound danger of stubborn unbelief starkly highlighted. Even miraculous healing does not guarantee that the recipient will believe in Jesus. Some who experience the healing power of Jesus are content with having their immediate plight resolved and disinterested in being saved from their sins and coming under his lordship. The man in John 5, despite his dramatic healing, sees no need to explore the identity of the One who healed him, caring only for his own self-comfort and interest.[9] The man in John 9, on the other hand, is changed not only on the outside, having seen the light of the sun for the first time in his life, but also on the inside as he sees "the Light" of the Son and responds with belief and worship (9:38). Similarly, the royal official experiences Jesus' supernatural intervention and believes. Three dramatic healings take place; two lead to faith, the other seemingly ends with no lasting spiritual impact.[10] How can this be? That is the question that the Gospel of John invites us to ponder. And in pondering it, we discover important lessons about discipleship from this character group.

Lessons in Discipleship: The Blind Man in John 9

There are many lessons in discipleship to be learned from the account of the healing of the blind man in John 9. We begin with a critical lesson that emerges from reading this account alongside the earlier healing account in John 5. Although both of the healed individuals had the opportunities for a new start in life and to become children of God by believing in Jesus (1:12), only one responded with belief. This narrative contrast is intended to help us keep the nature of physical healing in perspective. Physical healing, as dramatic and wonderful as it may be, if it is not accompanied by faith in Jesus, it is ultimately "fruitless and ineffectual," since "eventually the person will still die."[11] Only by receiving the Healer himself as Lord can eternal life be received and fear of death be removed forever.

Second, we cannot help but notice the development of the man's understanding of Jesus' identity and the parallel growth of his faith. At first,

---

9. Köstenberger, *Theology of John's Gospel*, 224.
10. For more, see Keener, *Gospel of John*, 1:639–40, and Köstenberger, *John*, 181–84.
11. Köstenberger, *Theology of John's Gospel*, 225.

when Jesus tells him to go to the pool of Siloam and wash, the blind man probably knew little about Jesus' identity, though he had almost certainly heard about the miracles Jesus had been doing. Like Rahab the prostitute in Joshua 2, who had only heard of the power of the God of Israel and chose to respond accordingly, the blind man does the same. He follows Jesus' command, perhaps hoping that the stories he had heard about "the man called Jesus" (9:11) were true. Following his healing, though, the man quickly comes to a new conclusion about Jesus and tells the Jewish authorities that Jesus must be a prophet (9:17). This level of comprehension about Jesus' identity is likely based on Hebrew prophets like Elijah and Elisha, who had also performed many miracles, some of which involved unusual rituals and required obedience to their commands for someone to be healed (see, e.g., 2 Kgs 5:5–15).[12] Making mud from spit, rubbing it in his eyes, and then telling him to go wash in order to be healed was consistent with the miraculous deeds of the prophets of old. Like the Samaritan woman (cf. 4:19), the healed man perceives that Jesus must be a prophet, but his growth in understanding does not stop there, nor does his growth toward discipleship.

When the man is brought for a second time to be interrogated before the religious leaders, the Pharisees believed that they could pressure him into confessing his sin and denying that Jesus could be from God. Their command for the man to "give glory to God" was likely an idiom exhorting him to confess his sin, just as it was in Joshua's command to Achan (Josh 7:19).[13] As readers, though, we already know that the man's former blindness had nothing to do with his personal sin (9:3) and he knew it too. So, rather than confessing his sin and condemning Jesus, he confessed the truth of what Jesus had done for him (9:25). He then went on to proclaim that Jesus had clearly come from God (9:33) and he invited the Pharisees to become his disciples (9:27). The man's verbal confessions before the Jewish authorities thus continue to reveal his developing perception of Jesus' true identity and his progression of faith. Finally, when he later encounters Jesus again, the eyes of his understanding are fully opened and he makes his final climactic display of discipleship with his confession of faith and act of worship (9:38).

By paralleling the blind man's progressive understanding of Jesus' identity with the simultaneous growth of his faith, John has created a

---

12. See also Reimer, "Man Born Blind," 434.

13. See Beasley-Murray, *John*, 158; Carson, *Gospel According to John*, 372; Bennema, *Encountering Jesus*, 252.

The Healing of the Blind Man

wonderful example of the redemptive effects of the gospel upon those who encounter and embrace Jesus. The formerly blind man's response of faith becomes a model of the conversion that anyone experiences when they embrace the lordship of Jesus, confess "I believe," and worship him (9:38).

Third, we see from John 9 that spiritual life flows out of obedience to Jesus. The blind man could have said, "Jesus, I believe you can heal me!" But that would not have been enough. He could have said, "Jesus, I believe you are the Messiah!" But that would not have been enough either. He was healed because he believed and *acted on that belief*. Disciples are careful to make sure that they not only understand what Jesus teaches them through all of Scripture, but they are also careful to respond appropriately to what Jesus teaches. For, it is only then that they can experience the wholeness and life that Jesus brings to his genuine disciples: "he went and washed and came back able to see" (9:7).

Unlike the healed blind man, the healed lame man in John 5 failed to follow Jesus and was apparently disinterested in his exhortation to repent (5:14–15). He was satisfied with physical healing and that was all he received. The formerly blind man, on the other hand, embraced Jesus as the Messiah and found life through him. He thus serves as a model for disciples today, showing us that true disciples grow in their devotion to Jesus and increasingly bow to him as Lord in all areas of their life. Many today profess to know God through Jesus, but do not follow him. The contrast that we see between the two healed men in John 5 and John 9 should lead us to question whether such people are disciples of Jesus at all. After all, the apostle John will later go on to write:

> "If we say that we have fellowship with him while we are walking in darkness, we lie and do not do what is true." (1 John 1:6)

> "Whoever says, 'I have come to know him,' but does not obey his commandments, is a liar, and in such a person the truth does not exist." (1 John 2:4)

Fourth, the healed blind man models what it looks like to tell others about Jesus, even those who appear to have far more religious expertise than the one bearing witness. He could have remained mute, viewing himself as "unqualified" to speak to such experts. Instead, he told them what Jesus had done for him and was courageous enough to point out obvious spiritual lessons. Every genuine disciple of Jesus today is already equipped to do the same.

Fifth, the formerly blind man's response to Jesus' question ("Do you believe in the Son of Man?") reinforces a central feature of discipleship in the Gospel of John: "And who is he, sir? Tell me, so that I may believe in him" (9:36). A disciple of Jesus embraces all that he teaches and acts on it. Or, to use the language of Jesus, anyone who is truly his disciple "continues in his word" (8:31). And those who continue in his word "will know the truth, and the truth will make [them] free" (8:32). That was precisely the experience of the blind man. He surrendered his will to Jesus and chose to embrace what Jesus said as truth. Jesus revealed himself as the Messiah and the man believed (knew the truth) and worshiped him. It was not simply his physical blindness that had given way to sight, but also his spiritual blindness that had been cured. The truth had set him free as he chose the path of a disciple.

Sixth, we dare not miss the cost of discipleship that is portrayed in this passage. The man born blind was immediately tested and persecuted after his healing. He found himself questioned by the religious leaders not once but twice, and he was ultimately kicked out of the synagogue. Disciples of Jesus will regularly face situations where they must choose whether to acknowledge or deny their allegiance to him. And the choice to acknowledge Jesus may well bring persecution or rejection. Later in John's Gospel, Jesus will warn those who follow him that they should expect persecution to come because of their faith in him (15:20). In the Synoptic Gospels, Jesus warns, "Everyone therefore who acknowledges me before others, I also will acknowledge before my Father in heaven; but whoever denies me before others, I also will deny before my Father in heaven" (Matt 10:32–33). In John 9, the man born blind becomes an important model of what this looks like and what publicly acknowledging Jesus might cost. Disciples today need to be aware that the longer they follow Jesus, the more they will be faced with decisions that may require them to sacrifice things that this world values (jobs, security, relationships) for the sake of their devotion to him. A growing disciple of Jesus will be increasingly willing to pay whatever price is necessary to live for the glory of God.

Lessons in Discipleship: Jesus in John 9

John 9 also teaches us some important lessons in discipleship through the words and actions of Jesus himself. First, this passage pushes us to recognize that disciples should not shy away from the truth that God can use

The Healing of the Blind Man

troubles in our lives as opportunities to show his good work and bring him glory (9:3). God's wonderful works can often be most vividly displayed in the midst of our own trials. Many disciples of Jesus today are fond of quoting a verse that perhaps we do not reflect on enough: "We know that all things work together for good for those who love God, who are called according to his purpose" (Rom 8:28). In the context, there is no question that "all things" is particularly focused on the trials and suffering we face in life. God will bring about good for us that glorifies him even in the midst of suffering. That should not surprise us. After all, the greatest suffering that anyone ever faced (Jesus' crucifixion) accomplished the greatest good the world has ever seen (the salvation of many) in the most perfect act of glorifying the Father ever known before or since (12:23; 13:31). Disciples need to realize that suffering and trials that we face can still be used by God for his glory. If we are truly going to be Jesus' disciples, we must "continue in his word" (8:31). And continuing in his word involves embracing all that he teaches as truth, even those things that we may find difficult to accept.

Second, notice how Jesus includes his disciples in his statement, "*We* must work the works of him who sent me while it is day; night is coming when no one can work" (9:4).[14] Jesus' *resolute focus* on accomplishing God's calling to die on the cross as the Lamb of God who would take away the sins of the world (1:29, 35) is thus presented as a model for his followers. They, too, need to seize the opportunities that God gives them, while there is still time. The original readers of the Gospel of John almost certainly would have not only remembered Jesus' words in 8:12 ("I am the light of the world. Whoever follows me will never walk in darkness but will have the light of life"), but would have also been familiar with his words recorded in Matt 5:14: "You are the light of the world." As they heard that night was coming (9:4), they would have recognized that there was great urgency for Jesus' disciples to let their light shine before others (Matt 5:16), while there was still the opportunity.

Third, the Gospel of John portrays Jesus as being "full of grace and truth" (1:14). Look at the grace that he shows to the healed man in 9:35: "Jesus heard that they had driven him out, and when he found him, he said, 'Do you believe in the Son of Man?'" The man born blind had been healed, but he was still lost. Jesus was not content that the blind man could now see. He recognized that this man still had a desperate spiritual need. So, what

---

14. Some ancient scribes wrote "I," rather than "we" here, but Jesus most likely said "we."

did Jesus do? He graciously went and found him! This is a model for Jesus' disciples who have been commissioned by him (Matt 28:19–20) to seek out those who do not yet know him. That task must be accomplished while there is still light (9:4). Disciples dare not be content with simply meeting the physical needs of those to whom they minister. Even for someone to be healed after four decades of blindness is nothing, if that person remains spiritually blind.

Finally, Jesus' statement at the end of the passage, "I came into this world for judgment so that those who do not see may see, and those who do see may become blind" (9:39), also teaches us an important lesson about discipleship. The Gospel of John frequently emphasizes God's gracious invitation to all to believe in Jesus and receive the gift of eternal life:

> "But to all who received him, who believed in his name, he gave power to become children of God." (1:12)

> "For God so loved the world that he gave his only Son, so that everyone who believes in him may not perish but may have eternal life." (3:16)

> "This is indeed the will of my Father, that all who see the Son and believe in him may have eternal life; and I will raise them up on the last day." (6:40)

> "Very truly, I tell you, whoever believes has eternal life." (6:47)

Notice the language in these passages: "all" (1:12), "everyone" (3:16), "all" (6:40), "whoever" (6:47). These and many other passages in the Gospel of John make it clear that God is inviting everyone to come to Jesus to receive life through him. Each of these passages, though, also makes it clear that it is only those who respond to God's invitation with appropriate belief in Jesus who will receive life (cf. 3:18). The account of the healing of the man born blind could have concluded at 9:38 and those reading this story would have gotten the point that we should imitate the healed man's response to Jesus: believe in him and worship him. That point, though, is dramatically strengthened by including a vivid picture of the alternative. Those who refuse to believe in Jesus willfully choose to remain spiritually blind (9:39). By claiming to see, they remain stuck in their sins (9:41).

In the end, the story of the healing of the man born blind in John 9 serves as a beautiful display of what occurs when someone is receptive to the gospel message. Every human being, like the man in this story, is born spiritually blind. They live in darkness and are hopeless without the

The Healing of the Blind Man

illumination that only God can provide. When people acknowledge their own blindness and their desperate need for God, though, God graciously sends his light, which penetrates the darkness in their lives and enables them to truly see.[15] When that happens, they experience what the prophet Isaiah so vividly describes: "the people who walked in darkness have seen a great light; those who lived in a land of deep darkness—on them light has shined" (Isa 9:2).

Questions for Disciples

1. When you face trials in life, do you see them as opportunities for the works and power of God to be displayed in your life? Even as you pray for deliverance do you also pray for wisdom and insight to see how God wants to display his power and his glory in that situation?

2. How often are we, like the religious leaders in John 5 and 9, more concerned about being "right" than about the spiritual condition of the people around us?

3. What traditions do you cling to that might be keeping you from understanding what is important to God and be keeping you from knowing Jesus more deeply?

4. How was the response of the blind man different from the response of the Jewish leaders in this passage? To what degree is your response to Jesus similar to one or the other?

5. Have you faced situations where you were given the opportunity to either acknowledge or deny your relationship with Jesus? Have there been times when you were bold in telling others about Jesus? Have there been times when you were too fearful to tell others about Jesus? What led to either your boldness or your fear? How do you want to be more like the healed blind man?

---

15. See Bennema, *Encountering Jesus*, 255.

8

Mary and Martha, Mary and Judas
Faith, Devotion, and Fake Discipleship

THE NEXT MAJOR CHARACTERS introduced into the narrative are Mary and Martha, the sisters of Lazarus, in John 11. Through their distinctive interactions with Jesus, they form an obvious character pair from which we learn important lessons about discipleship. As we will see in John 12–13, however, a single character may be paired with more than one other character within the narrative. While John 11 presents Mary and Martha as contrasting characters, John 12–13 contrasts Mary with Judas.

Mary and Martha

The account of Mary and Martha's interaction with Jesus is found in 11:1–44. At the beginning of John 11, we learn of three individuals who were particularly close to Jesus: Martha, Mary, and Lazarus (11:3, 5). When Lazarus became seriously ill, Mary and Martha sent word to Jesus: "Lord, he whom you love is ill" (11:3). Christians today often assume that Jesus had twelve disciples, but no real friends. After all, how could God incarnate have human friends? This passage, along with all the references to "the disciple whom Jesus loved" in the Gospel of John, reminds us that just like most human beings, Jesus had certain individuals to whom he was particularly close.

Martha is the first to encounter Jesus in the narrative. Jesus had been told that his close friend Lazarus was ill (11:3). After delaying going to help Lazarus (11:6), Jesus eventually told his disciples that Lazarus had died and then they left for Bethany (11:14–15). When he arrived, he discovered that Lazarus has been in the tomb for four days (11:17). Jews of that time would have typically buried a dead person on the day of their death and then mourned for them for six more days at their home.[1] Relatives and friends would come to their home to comfort and mourn with them. This helps us understand why Mary stayed behind when Martha went to meet Jesus (11:20). Normally, Martha would not have left the house. She would have expected Jesus, like others, to come to her. By leaving her house and going to meet Jesus, Martha shows him great honor. Mary, on the other hand, remains at home, not because she loved Jesus any less, but in order to welcome visitors who continued to arrive at their home.

In 11:17–27, before Jesus says or does anything, Martha demonstrates some of the most remarkable faith of anyone in all of Scripture. She expresses not only her belief that Jesus could have prevented her brother's death, but also shows astounding faith by believing that even after Lazarus's death, it was still not too late for Jesus to intervene: "Lord, if you had been here, my brother would not have died. But even now I know that God will give you whatever you ask of him" (11:21–22). Lazarus had been dead four days! He was not "mostly dead." He was completely dead. Martha knew that his body would already be decomposing (11:39), but that did not mean that it was too late for Jesus to save Lazarus. She had never seen or heard of someone being raised from the dead after three days in a tomb, but she believed that Jesus could do it. There is even more to Martha's faith, though. When Jesus asks her if she believes that everyone who believes in him will never die (11:25–26), Martha responds that she believes that Jesus is the Messiah (11:27). She thus illustrates the saving belief that leads to someone becoming a child of God (1:12).

In the next part of the passage, 11:28–37, we encounter Martha's sister Mary. After Jesus had finished his conversation with Martha, he sent Martha home and instructed her to send Mary to him. Like Martha, Mary shows faith that Jesus could have prevented Lazarus's death: "When Mary came where Jesus was and saw him, she knelt at his feet and said to him, 'Lord, if you had been here, my brother would not have died'" (11:32). It is worth noting that in the Gospels, Mary is often found at the feet of Jesus. In Luke 10, she is sitting at Jesus' feet; in John 11, she is crying at Jesus' feet; and in John 12, she is anointing Jesus' feet. In each case, she adopts a position of humility and devotion. In this passage, both Martha and Mary

---

1. Keener, *Gospel of John*, 2:842.

express their love for and faith in Jesus, one by a verbal confession and the other by a physical act of devotion.[2]

Mary's faith in Jesus is real, but as part of a character pair, we immediately notice that there is a contrast between her faith and the faith of Martha. Mary loves Jesus and knows that he could have saved Lazarus from dying, but she has not yet realized, as Martha has, that even now Jesus could rescue Lazarus from the grave. She had apparently not yet come to realize that God would do whatever Jesus asked (11:22). And she apparently did not yet recognize, as Martha did, that Jesus was "the Messiah, the Son of God, the one coming into the world" (11:27).[3]

Lessons in Discipleship: Mary and Martha in John 11

There are a number of obvious lessons we learn from the characters of Mary and Martha in John 11. From both sisters we learn a simple lesson in 11:1–3. When we face profound trials in life, the answer is always the same: Take our cares to Jesus. Go to the one who cares for us: "Cast all your anxiety on him, because he cares for you" (1 Pet 5:7). We need to remind ourselves that God has redeemed us with the blood of his beloved Son and that has profound implications for how he will care for us in our times of need: "He who did not withhold his own Son, but gave him up for all of us, will he not with him also give us everything else?" (Rom 8:32).

From Martha, we also see a picture of how a disciple takes action even in their deepest sorrow. Martha would have still been grief-stricken. And her culture would have led her to feel obligated to stay at home to allow others to share in her mourning. She recognized, however, that the appropriate response to Jesus was to put his honor above her grief and above cultural expectations. And so, she went to meet him. Disciples today need to be

---

2. Collins, "'Who Are You?'" 80–84. Collins emphasizes the use of contrast between the characters of Mary and Martha in John's Gospel. Collins contends that John highlights his contrast of the two sisters by their spatial separation from one another in the stories. This separation underscores differences between the two sisters, such as Martha's use of words in her confession of Jesus (11:27) versus Mary's action of devotion by kneeling at the feet of Jesus (11:32). Culpepper also notes the contrast between the personalities of the two sisters as "Martha is the one with discerning faith," while Mary "represents the response of devotion and uncalculatingly, extravagant love, and in contrast to her sister never verbalizing her faith in Jesus." Culpepper, *Anatomy*, 141–42.

3. It is important to avoid reading John's account through the lens of Luke 10:38–42. Otherwise, we might begin with a negative opinion of Martha and miss the positive lessons that this narrative reveals through her.

quick to discern when Jesus takes priority over important areas of life and to take action.

From Martha, we are also reminded that disciples who recognize that Jesus is the Messiah also understand that no matter how impossible the situation might be, Jesus has the power to intervene. Although we are not explicitly told this in John 11, Martha appears to recognize that Jesus is far more than a political deliverer. Although she might not yet acknowledge his deity (1:1), she does understand that, as the Messiah, he has the right to ask God for anything (11:22). In her situation, he was even able to bring life where there was death. That is the faith that every disciple of Jesus is called to embrace and enjoy. Accepting Jesus as the Messiah leads to a life where no situation is ever hopeless or beyond God's intervention.

Finally, we also discover in Martha an example of a disciple who was quick to believe and embrace whatever Jesus told her, regardless of how unlikely it might have seemed from a logical perspective (11:23–27). This again reminds us of the truth of Jesus' words in 8:31–32: "If you continue in my word, you are truly my disciples; and you will know the truth, and the truth will make you free." Martha chose to continue in Jesus' words and by doing so she experienced the truth of what he had said in a profound way (her brother is raised from the dead!). And she experienced the freedom of living under the lordship of Jesus Christ.

There are also lessons to learn from the character of Mary. Although the character pair of Martha and Mary clearly serves to contrast their responses to Jesus, Mary's faith is not portrayed in negative terms. She is quick to respond to Jesus' summons (11:28–29). She demonstrated her devotion to Jesus in a tangible way (11:32). And she had clearly come to believe that Jesus was fully capable of preventing death (11:32). These are all characteristics of a genuine disciple. What we find in the narrative, though, is that Mary's faith was not yet as robust as her sister's. By pairing her with her sister Martha in this narrative, the apostle John effectively encourages us to aspire to a faith that sees Jesus as more than someone who can help us in times of sickness or trouble. He is more than a healer. He is the Messiah, the Son of God. And as the Son of God, he has power not only over sickness, but over life and death itself.

Lessons in Discipleship: Jesus in John 11

In addition to the ways in which Mary and Martha model discipleship in John 11, we also discover some striking lessons from Jesus himself. First,

The Making of a Disciple

remember, Jesus was particularly close to Mary, Martha, and Lazarus. He loved them! And yet, "after having heard that Lazarus was ill, he stayed two days longer in the place where he was" (11:6). Jesus was well aware that waiting two extra days would create suffering for his friends, yet he deliberately stayed away. Why? Because he knew that Lazarus's death would not be the end of his story. In fact, Lazarus's imminent death would be "for God's glory, so that the Son of God may be glorified through it" (11:5). There is no question that the death of Lazarus would not only have been extremely painful for Mary and Martha (not to mention Lazarus himself), but also for Jesus. Nevertheless, Jesus models for us that God can take what the devil intended to harm us and bring great good out of it, just as he did with Jesus' crucifixion. What would happen if followers of Jesus today would begin to look at their trials and even intense seasons of suffering as opportunities for God to reveal himself to them and to the world around them in profound, life-changing ways? If Lazarus had never died, Martha would have never witnessed Jesus bringing him back to life! Her view of Jesus would have been much more limited, much *smaller*. Now, that she had witnessed the glory of God and the goodness and power of Jesus in an undeniable way she would never be the same.

Second, we cannot help but notice Jesus' compassion for others and his lack of concern for his own welfare in this passage. Although Jesus allowed Lazarus to die, he still intervened to rescue Lazarus from death, even when his own life was on the line. After waiting two days, he told his disciples that they were going back to Judea in order for him to help Lazarus, despite the fact that the Jewish leaders had recently attempted to stone him there and were still seeking an opportunity to kill him (11:7–8). This was a dangerous mission on which Jesus was going to help his friend. So much so that Thomas, in urging the other disciples to be courageous and accompany Jesus expresses it this way, "Let us also go, that we may die with him" (11:16). Those who follow Jesus must be prepared to put their own lives on the line to do the work to which God calls them.

Third, Jesus challenges Martha to grow in her faith beyond embracing the common belief in eschatological resurrection. He invites her to believe that he is the one who holds all life in his hands and he is perfectly capable of raising someone from the dead: "I am the resurrection and the life" (11:25). And how does Martha respond to Jesus' invitation? "Yes, Lord, I believe that you are the Messiah, the Son of God, the one coming into the world" (11:27).⁴ The life of a disciple of Jesus is all about encountering more and more revelation about who Jesus is, who the Father is, who the Holy Spirit is, and choosing to embrace and act on those beliefs. Martha models the proper response for each of us: "Yes, Lord, I believe!" (11:27).

Fourth, Jesus teaches us an important lesson about the glory of God in this passage. And it does not come simply through Jesus doing something that had never before been done in all of history. For God to receive glory, it had to be clear that God was doing the work. Look what Jesus does in 11:41–42. After the stone had been rolled away from the tomb where Lazarus had been buried, "Jesus looked upward and said, 'Father, I thank you for having heard me. I knew that you always hear me, but I have said this for the sake of the crowd standing here, so that they may believe that you sent me.'" Jesus prayed. Martha knew that God would do whatever Jesus asked (11:22) and Jesus wanted the crowd around him to know that God was the one empowering him to do what he was about to do. So, he prayed, and he did it publicly so that God would receive the glory and people would know that the Father had sent Jesus as they witnessed the miraculous sign of Lazarus being raised from the dead (11:41–42). Do you see the pattern that Jesus sets for his disciples here? The Father receives glory when Jesus' disciples publicly seek the Father's intervention in a particular situation. Some Christians refuse to ask God publicly to intervene in hopeless situations or, at best, they ask God to "guide the doctors' hands" or "help that aspirin to do its job." Jesus told his disciples, "Very truly, I tell you, the one who believes in me will also do the works that I do and, in fact, will do greater works than these, because I am going to the Father" (14:12). Disciples of Jesus should watch for opportunities to do such mighty works and be prepared to pray publicly for God's powerful intervention so that he can receive glory and those who do not know him can see his great power.

Mary and Judas

In John 12, the scene shifts, but the characters initially remain the same. This leads us as readers to watch for further character development. Jesus is back in Bethany and he is present at a dinner where Martha is serving

---

4. Interestingly, in John's Gospel, it is Martha who makes the confession of Jesus' messiahship associated with Peter in the Synoptics (cf. Mark 8:29; Matt 16:16; Luke 9:20). John does note, though, that Peter makes the similar statement that Jesus is "the Holy One of God" (6:69).

the meal and Lazarus is among those dining with Jesus (12:1–2). Having just read John 11, a careful reader naturally wonders, "Where is Mary?" We had seen Mary's act of devotion to Jesus in 11:32, as she went out to meet him and humbly fell at his feet. Now, we find her taking her devotion to an even more humble level. She takes some very expensive perfumed oil and uses it to anoint Jesus' feet. Then, she goes even deeper in her humble act of devotion and wipes his feet with her hair. This would have been shocking behavior in that cultural context.

Mary, though, is not the only major character in this scene. There is a second, besides Jesus himself: Judas Iscariot. When Judas sees what Mary has done, he is outraged: "Why was this perfume not sold for three hundred denarii and the money given to the poor?" (12:5). The apostle John then tells us, "He said this not because he cared about the poor, but because he was a thief; he kept the common purse and used to steal what was put into it." (12:6). We see an obvious contrast here between Mary and Judas, and the lessons we are supposed to learn from that contrast are driven home in part by Jesus' own assessment of Mary's actions in response to Judas's complaint: "Jesus said, 'Leave her alone. She bought it so that she might keep it for the day of my burial. You always have the poor with you, but you do not always have me'" (12:7–8). In Jewish culture, before someone was buried, their body was first perfumed and wrapped in cloth (see 19:39–42). Mary's act, then, symbolized Jesus' approaching death and burial (12:7a). And to drive that point home, Jesus made it clear that he would not always be with them (12:7b).

Lessons in Discipleship: Mary and Judas in John 12

What can we learn from the contrasting character pair of Mary and Judas in this brief scene? The most prominent discipleship lesson relates to Mary's striking act of devotion. We had already seen Mary rushing to meet Jesus and falling down at his feet (11:31–32). Now, we find Mary showing the depth of her devotion to Jesus by doing something that Judas thought was outrageous. She gave her very best to Jesus. She gave Jesus something that was incredibly costly. More than that, the *way* that she offered her gift to Jesus was also striking. It was only slaves who washed people's feet. In fact, many Jews of the day insisted that only Gentile slaves should do this menial job because it would be too demeaning for a Jewish slave to be made to wash someone's feet.[5] And while it was honorable to anoint someone's head, anointing someone's feet showed your humble submission to that person. Wiping someone's feet with your hair was far beyond what was viewed as acceptable in that society. Mary's actions, then, serve as a dramatic act of devotion wrapped in absolute humility. In Thailand, someone addressing the king might say something like, "The top of my head (highest and most important part of the body) speaks to the bottom of your feet (the lowest and least important part of the body)." This is a way of highlighting how much more important the king is than the person who is addressing him. Mary's actions were similar as she anointed Jesus' feet and then wiped them with her hair. A woman's hair was her glory (1 Cor 11:7). Mary humbled herself before Jesus, and she also gave him her very best. She was not like Cain who simply brought some of the produce from his fields; she was like Abel who "brought of the *firstlings* of his flock, their *fat portions*" (Gen 4:4). She sought to bring a gift that would be appropriate for the value she placed on Jesus. This should be the focus and desire of every genuine disciple of Jesus.

There are also important lessons to be learned from Judas in this passage. Judas is identified as the one who would betray Jesus (12:4), but this passage shows us that Judas did not suddenly become a wicked man when he finally decided to betray Jesus. Rather, he had lived a life of secret sin even as he masqueraded as Jesus' disciple. He was a thief as well as Jesus' betrayer. And his pattern of sin may well have ultimately led him to betray Jesus altogether. In the end, Judas cared more about money than he cared about Jesus—he sold Jesus for thirty pieces of silver (Matt 26:15)!

It is worth emphasizing that John 13 points to the fact that none of the other disciples suspected Judas of being anything but loyal to Jesus (see 13:27–30). He appeared to be a godly follower of Jesus, but in Jesus' own words, he was "a devil" (6:70). This is a good reminder that appearances can be deceiving. To look like a disciple does not make one a disciple of Jesus. And a good self-test to discover whether or not you are masquerading as a disciple of Jesus emerges from the contrasting behaviors of Judas and Mary. Judas followed Jesus for what he could *get*. That is the mark of a false disciple. Mary, as a genuine disciple, was eager to *give* Jesus her greatest treasure. While we may have been left after reading John 11 thinking that Mary's faith was somehow defective, in John 12 we discover just how deep

---

5. Carson, *Gospel according to John*, 462.

Mary's devotion to Jesus was. She existed to serve Jesus. No sacrifice was too great to make for her beloved Master.

In the end, the character pairing of Mary and Judas invites us to examine our hearts and ask ourselves: Is my attitude toward Jesus more like Mary's or more like Judas's? Do I follow Jesus for what I can get or do I also follow him for what I can give to him? Do I only appear to be a disciple of Jesus, when the truth is that I am a lover of self, a lover or pleasure, or a lover or money, rather than a lover of God, "holding to the outward form of godliness but denying its power" (see 2 Tim 3:1–5)?

Lessons in Discipleship: Jesus in John 12

Even within this brief scene, we also find discipleship lessons coming from Jesus himself. Jesus teaches us an important lesson about priorities. He does not chastise Mary for her extravagant act of devotion to him. He embraces it, even at the expense of the poor. This reminds disciples of Jesus that the fact that we are called to love one another and care for those in need does not take away from our central calling to love God with all our heart, soul, and strength. This is what Mary was doing. She was giving her best to the Lord Jesus. And her act of extravagant devotion was pleasing to him. The same will always be true for Jesus' disciples today. Jesus is honored when our tangible devotion to him showcases his worth to us. Jesus was not embarrassed by Mary's "outrageous" display of affection. Just as parents are never embarrassed by their children's displays of love for them, but rather delight in such actions, so Jesus readily accepted Mary's act of devotion.

Questions for Disciples

1. Do you hesitate to take your practical needs to Jesus? Or, like Martha and Mary, are you quick to cast your cares on him and seek his help?
2. Do you allow cultural expectations, including church expectations, to keep you from pursuing help from God in times of challenging trials?
3. Are you facing a "hopeless" situation, like Martha and Mary were, that needs to be brought to God?
4. Are you quick to believe and act on whatever Jesus tells you to do and to believe in the Word of God?

5. Have you embraced the fact that your trials, even severe trials, are often the contexts where God is seeking to reveal his glory to you and to others through you?

6. Are you willing to take the "risk" of publicly seeking God's help in crisis situations, as Jesus modeled in John 11?

7. How does your visible devotion to Jesus compare to Mary's devotion to Jesus in John 12?

8. Are you a genuine disciple of Jesus like Mary or a fake disciple of Jesus like Judas? In what areas of your life are you secretly living in sin, like Judas was?

9. Are you, like Judas, more concerned with what you can get from Jesus? Or, like Mary, is your focus on what you can give to Jesus?

9

Peter and the Beloved Disciple

Passionate Devotion, Steady Devotion

WE HAVE SEEN HOW the apostle John creates character pairs by presenting major characters in close proximity within the narrative and linking them in a variety of ways. These pairings are typically in view in a particular part of the narrative only. In the case of Peter and the Beloved Disciple, on the other hand, we discover not only character development for each of them throughout the Gospel of John, but also character contrast as they periodically engage with Jesus in different ways within the same scene.

Beginning in John 13 we find several scenes that highlight differences between these two central characters. The "Beloved Disciple" or "the disciple whom Jesus loved" is a somewhat mysterious figure in the Gospel of John. Most scholars identify him as John, the son of Zebedee.[1] We learn in 21:20–24 that the Beloved Disciple was the author of the Gospel of John. So, why does the Beloved Disciple never identify himself directly? Ultimately, we do not know. He may have chosen to downplay his identity out of humility, out of a desire to keep the focus on Jesus, or perhaps to present himself as a model of what true discipleship looks like without drawing attention to himself as a person.[2]

---

1. Some scholars have made the argument that Lazarus may be a more likely candidate for the Beloved Disciple, since he is explicitly mentioned in the text as one who was loved by Jesus (11:3). For more, see Witherington, *What Have They Done to Jesus?* 146. See also Keener, *Gospel of John*, 1:86.

2. Culpepper notes that "the Beloved Disciple was a real historical person who has representative, paradigmatic, or symbolic significance in John. In this he is unlike the other Johannine characters only in that he is the ideal disciple, the paradigm of

Peter and the Beloved Disciple

Whatever the case, "the disciple whom Jesus loved" (13:23; 19:6; 20:2; 21:7, 20) is an interesting title. Obviously, Jesus loved all of his disciples (cf. 15:9, 12), but he still had an inner circle of disciples who were the only ones present with him on some important occasions: Peter, James, and John (see, e.g., Matt 17:1//Mark 9:2//9:28; Mark 5:37; 14:33; Luke 8:51). And among this inner circle, John seems to have been particularly close to Jesus, as is suggested not only by this title, but also by his position at the Last Supper (13:22) and the fact that he is the one to whom Jesus entrusts the care of his mother after his death (19:26–27). It is, therefore, not surprising that the Beloved Disciple comes out looking more like an ideal disciple than Peter does in the Gospel of John.

The first scene that we will consider, in which the characters of Peter and the Beloved Disciple are paired, is found in 13:1–38, where the first part of Jesus' final evening with his disciples is described. At the beginning of this scene, Jesus does an audacious thing. He takes on the role of the lowest of slaves and proceeds to wash his disciples' feet. We do not know how many of the disciples had already had their feet washed by the time Jesus came to Peter (13:5), but the text leaves us with the impression that they submitted to Jesus' actions. When Jesus came to Peter, on the other hand, Peter was appalled at the thought of Jesus doing such a thing for him (13:6) and he refused to go along with what Jesus intended: "You will never wash my feet" (13:8). Jesus then told Peter that if he did not wash him, Peter would have no part with him, no share in eternal fellowship with Jesus.[3] At this point, Peter realized his mistake and asked Jesus to wash his hands and his head as well as his feet (13:9). He thus ultimately showed submission to Jesus, but he also showed misunderstanding. So, Jesus reminded Peter that those who have already bathed (at a public bath and then returned home) only needed to wash their feet to be completely clean again (13:10).

This episode clearly shows Peter as one who is sincere and earnest, but who also lacks insight and comprehension into the spiritual things that Jesus is trying to teach him. Indeed, his actions and words clearly point to the fact that Peter thought he knew better than Jesus at times! And this was not the first time Peter had made this mistake:

---

discipleship. He has no misunderstandings." Culpepper, *Anatomy*, 121. See also Collins, "From John to the Beloved Disciple," 359–69. Some scholars reject the notion that the Beloved Disciple serves as the epitome of discipleship. See, e.g., Bauckham, who sees the Beloved Disciple not as an ideal disciple but as an ideal witness. Bauckham, *Testimony of the Beloved Disciple*, 82–85. See also Bennema, *Encountering Jesus*, 309–14.

3. Keener, *Gospel of John*, 2:909.

The Making of a Disciple

> Then he began to teach them that the Son of Man must undergo great suffering, and be rejected by the elders, the chief priests, and the scribes, and be killed, and after three days rise again. He said all this quite openly. And Peter took him aside and began to rebuke him. But turning and looking at his disciples, he rebuked Peter and said, "Get behind me, Satan! For you are setting your mind not on divine things but on human things." (Mark 8:31–33)

We will come back to the lessons that God is teaching us through Peter's actions in this passage a bit later. For now, it is important to notice how the narrative spotlight is placed on Peter through his words, actions, and interactions with Jesus in this passage.

Immediately, after washing his disciples' feet, Jesus told his disciples that one of them was going to betray him (13:18–21). Since Peter wanted to find out who Jesus was talking about, but did not want to shout such a sensitive question to him across the room, he motioned to the Beloved Disciple, who was eating next to Jesus, to ask the Lord to which disciple he was referring (13:23). This is the first mention of the disciple "whom Jesus loved" in John's Gospel.[4] As readers of the Gospel of John, such a title should grab our attention. The title, in and of itself, puts a spotlight on this character each time he appears in the narrative. It raises the question: Why did Jesus love this particular disciple in a special way? And it leads us to be attentive to this disciple's behavior in an effort to discover the answer to that question. In this particular scene, we find the Beloved Disciple simply asking Jesus who the betrayer was and Jesus telling him that it was the one to whom he would give a piece of bread after he had dipped it into a dish (Judas Iscariot, 13:25).

To understand this scene, we need to recognize that having a meal in the ancient world looked very different than it does today. We often think of Jesus sitting at a large table with his disciples, like we see in Leonardo DaVinci's depiction of the Last Supper. In Jesus' culture, though, people did not eat sitting in chairs at a table. Instead, they typically reclined on low couches, or on mats on the floor, and ate from a low table. They would support themselves by leaning on their left elbow with their heads toward the table, while they ate with their right hands. When eating, then, they would have someone lying directly behind them and someone lying directly in front of them in the same position, with three persons typically sharing

---

4. Beck observes: "There is no introduction to detail anything of his personality traits, background, family, or the circumstances which led to his following Jesus. He is simply stated to be 'one of his disciples'" (13:23). Beck, "Whom Jesus Loved," 225.

the same couch. At the meal scene in John 13, the Beloved Disciple had the position in front of Jesus. So, all he had to do was to lean his head back or turn his head slightly and his head would be very close to Jesus. Whether or not this was the Beloved Disciple's usual place at a meal, we do not know; but his close proximity to Jesus in this scene fits with his description, "the disciple whom Jesus loved." And in this scene, his privileged position gave him close access to Jesus that Peter did not have.[5]

Later in John 13, Jesus tells his disciples that he will soon be departing and that where he is going, they will not be able to follow (13:33). At this point, Peter again shows his lack of understanding of Jesus' mission as he asks where Jesus is going (13:36). When Jesus tells him that where he is going Peter will not be able to follow, Peter insists that he will do whatever it takes to follow Jesus, even if it requires him to lay down his life for him (13:37). In other words, Peter declares his absolute devotion to Jesus no matter what it may cost him. Peter's overconfident pronouncement of loyalty, though, leads Jesus to reveal that not only will one of his followers betray him to the Jewish authorities, but Peter himself will abandon him: "Will you lay down your life for me? Very truly, I tell you, before the cock crows, you will have denied me three times" (13:38). This is a shocking scene. And the nature of this scene once again places the spotlight on Peter, inviting readers to consider what lessons about discipleship they are intended to learn from this important character.

After his "Farewell Discourse" to his disciples in John 14–16 and his "High Priestly Prayer" for his disciples in John 17, Jesus led his disciples across the Kidron Valley to a garden, which is identified in the Synoptic Gospels as Gethsemane. There a detachment of Roman soldiers, together with Jewish police, arrived to arrest Jesus. Once again, the narrative spotlight turns for a moment to Peter. Jesus was in danger. So, Peter drew his sword and took a swing at the person closest to him. The fact that he cut off the ear of the high priest's slave (18:10) makes it clear that Peter meant business. Once again, though, Jesus indicated that Peter had misunderstood his mission: "Jesus said to Peter, 'Put your sword back into its sheath. Am I not to drink the cup that the Father has given me?'" (18:11). Jesus had repeatedly told his disciples that he was going to Jerusalem to die, but Peter had still not grasped or embraced Jesus' mission.

---

5. Resseguie notes that Peter represents the point of view of the disciples who miss the deeper significance of Jesus' words and actions, while "the Beloved Disciple sees what other disciples do not see and represents this ideal point of view in the narrative." Resseguie, "Beloved Disciple," 540.

After Jesus' arrest, we see Peter and another disciple, who is generally thought to be the Beloved Disciple, follow Jesus to the high priest's courtyard (18:15).[6] Here, the Beloved Disciple's social status is contrasted with Peter. The fact that the Beloved Disciple "was known to the high priest" suggests a more prominent place in society than Peter enjoyed. Peter, on the other hand, is forced to wait outside until the Beloved Disciple vouches for him and he is allowed inside as well (18:15–16). The focus then shifts to Peter who was warming himself by a charcoal fire (18:18, 25). We find Peter being asked three times if he was one of Jesus' disciples and denying it every time (18:17, 25–27), just as Jesus had predicted.[7]

Our next encounter with one of these two characters is at Jesus' crucifixion (19:25–27). This is the only scene in the Gospel of John where the Beloved Disciple is named and Peter is absent. Peter's absence, though, itself speaks volumes. It reminds us that Peter, along with the rest of the Twelve, had abandoned Jesus at his darkest hour. Only one of the Twelve had apparently remained true to Jesus, the Beloved Disciple. And now, as Jesus hung on the cross, one of the last things he did before his death was to tell his mother who was standing next to the Beloved Disciple, "Woman, here is your son." And he says to the Beloved Disciple, "Here is your mother" (19:26–27). We cannot help, at this point, but remember that Jesus' brothers did not yet believe in him (7:5); so, Jesus entrusted the care of his mother to the person closest to him who did believe in him.

The next scene where we encounter Peter and the Beloved Disciple is immediately after Jesus' resurrection. Mary Magdalene, the first witness to Jesus' empty tomb (20:1), runs to share the news of what she had seen with Peter and the Beloved Disciple (20:2), which again underscores the standing of these two disciples in the Gospel of John and brings them back

---

6. That this other disciple is the Beloved Disciple is supported in 20:2 when "the other disciple" is identified as the disciple whom Jesus loved using the definite article ("the other disciple"), which very likely points back to the "other disciple" here in 18:15. See Resseguie, "Beloved Disciple," 541; Brown, *Gospel According to John*, 822; Beasley-Murray, *John*, 324.

7. Resseguie, "Beloved Disciple," 543. As Peter is outside denying that he knows Jesus, Jesus is inside being tried by the Jewish leaders. The interlocking of parallel stories (Jesus' trial versus Peter's "trial") is developed with an A, B, A', B' pattern in the text, moving back and forth between the events with Peter and Jesus respectively, that invites comparison and contrast between the two "trials." While Jesus is inside confessing truth, Peter is outside denying truth. Brown aptly states: "John has constructed a dramatic contrast wherein Jesus stands up to his questioners and denies nothing, while Peter cowers before his questioners and denies everything." Brown, *Gospel According to John*, 842.

into the narrative spotlight. Mary's assumption that his body had been stolen causes both disciples to run to the tomb to investigate (20:3). We then find an interesting comment from the narrator: "The two were running together, but the other disciple outran Peter and reached the tomb first" (20:4). This seemingly arbitrary detail regarding the ability of the Beloved Disciple to run faster than Peter likely, as some have suggested, highlights his devotion to Jesus through his eagerness to discover what has happened.[8] We will later see Peter responding to Jesus in a similar way (21:7).

The Beloved Disciple reached the tomb first and looked in, but he did not enter. Then Peter, who regularly rushed to speak or take action when others might hesitate, entered the tomb and inspected the abandoned linen wrappings (20:6–7). Only then did the Beloved Disciple enter the tomb and when he did, "he saw and believed" (20:8). We are reminded in 20:9 that even up until this point in Jesus' ministry, his disciples "did not understand the Scripture, that he must rise from the dead." This statement serves to highlight the Beloved Disciple as not only the first to reach the tomb, but also the first disciple to grasp that Jesus had to die and rise from the dead.

Finally, in the last chapter of the Gospel of John, Jesus appears once again to his disciples as they are fishing at the Sea of Tiberius (Galilee). While scholars tend to view this chapter as an epilogue, it effectively serves to complete the unfinished portrait of discipleship that John has been painting. It is thus a crucial part of the Gospel of John. It presents us with another fascinating series of scenes that are found only in John's Gospel. In the first scene, we find a group of Jesus' disciples, including Peter and the Beloved Disciple, still in a boat after a night of fruitless fishing (21:1–3). It is just after daybreak and the risen Jesus is standing on the beach (21:4). He asks the disciples if they have caught anything (21:5). At this point, they have no idea that it is Jesus who is shouting to them. When they tell him that they have caught nothing at all, Jesus instructs them to cast their nets on the right side of the boat and they proceed to haul in a massive catch of fish (21:6). Not surprisingly, given what we have seen thus far in the Gospel of John, the Beloved Disciple once again shows spiritual perception and is the first to recognize Jesus: "It is the Lord!" (21:7). When Peter hears from the Beloved Disciple that it was Jesus on the shore, he responds as he has always responded, with action. He jumps out of the boat and swims to shore, leaving the other disciples to row the boat to shore dragging the net full of fish.

---

8. See Byrne, "Faith of the Beloved Disciple," 86.

The Making of a Disciple

Once on shore, Jesus tells the disciples to bring some of their fish to the fire he had burning (21:9). Then, we find the famous final scene between Peter and Jesus. After eating together, Jesus asked Peter, "do you love me more than these?" Peter responded, "Yes, Lord; you know that I love you." Jesus then told him, "Feed my lambs" (21:15). Jesus asked Peter the same question two additional times, and after each affirmative answer, Jesus followed up in the same way: "tend my sheep," "feed my sheep" (21:16, 17). Although preachers have tended to focus on the different words for "love" in this dialogue,[9] the focus of the passage is on Jesus repeating the same question three times in response to Peter's three earlier denials of Jesus in John 18. In doing so, Jesus gives Peter an opportunity to undo his earlier threefold denial by affirming three times his devotion to Jesus.[10]

After Jesus reaffirms (and reinstates) Peter as his disciple and gives him a commission to shepherd his flock, he prophesies that when Peter is older, his hands will be stretched out and he will be taken to a place where he does not want to go (21:18). John tells us that Jesus said this to "indicate the kind of death by which he [Peter] would glorify God" (21:19).[11] Peter had earlier pledged that he was ready to follow Jesus to his death, but he was unable to carry through with his vow when given the opportunity (13:36–38; 18:15–17). Now, Jesus assures Peter that in the future, he will willingly follow him to the cross.[12] Jesus, though, also wants to make it clear that despite this prophecy about his death, Peter should not focus on dying, but rather on how he should live: "Follow me" (21:19).

It is at this point that the Beloved Disciple returns to the stage, though the spotlight remains on Peter. We are told that Peter "turned and saw the disciple whom Jesus loved following them" (21:20). And "when Peter saw him, he said to Jesus, 'Lord, what about him?'" (21:21). Peter had just learned that he would be crucified in the future. Now, he wondered what would happen to the Beloved Disciple. Jesus responded: "If it is my will that he remain until I come, what is that to you? Follow me!" (21:22).

---

9. The Greek words actually both mean the same thing. This is very likely just a case of stylistic variation.

10. See the discussion in Burge, *John*, 586–88.

11. According to early Christian tradition, Peter was later crucified on a cross as a martyr in Rome (*Acts Pet.* 36–41; Tertullian *Scorp.* 15:3; Eusebius *Hist. eccl.* 2.25.8, 3.1.2). Following the logic of the narrative, Jesus essentially tells Peter that at the right time he "will become a good shepherd by imitating Jesus' death: 'the good shepherd lays down his life for the sheep' (10:11)." Labahn, "Simon Peter," 165.

12. See Bennema, *Encountering Jesus*, 121.

Lessons in Discipleship: Peter

We learn a variety of lessons as we consider Peter's actions in the Gospel of John and compare and contrast his actions with those of the Beloved Disciple in John 13–21. In the foot-washing scene in John 13, Peter demonstrates a common trait among those struggling to grow as disciples of Jesus. Rather than simply submitting to Jesus, Peter attempted to correct Jesus: "Peter said to him, 'You will never wash my feet'" (John 13:8). Like Peter, disciples today sometimes think they know better than God what their lives should look like or how God should behave or how he should respond to their prayers or change their circumstances. Peter needed to be corrected and so do we, because failure to submit to what God says in his Word is a serious matter: "Jesus answered, 'Unless I wash you, you have no share with me'" (13:9). To belong to Jesus, by definition, involves submitting to what he says, whether it makes sense to us or not.

The lesson for us in Peter's actions in the foot-washing scene, though, is not complete. Notice how Peter responds to Jesus' correction: "Simon Peter said to him, "Lord, not my feet only but also my hands and my head!'" (13:10). Jesus corrects; Peter repents and reaffirms his absolute devotion to him. This is the mark of a growing disciple. As disciples of Jesus read the Word of God or listen to it preached or taught, they should expect to have their areas of wrong thinking and wrong living corrected. All of us presently "see dimly" (1 Cor 13:12); all of us are works in progress; all of us tend to have at least partially distorted views of God and his ways. Are we open to correction? Are we eager for correction? When corrected, do we respond like Peter with an absolute willingness to be fully corrected and to change our thinking or change our ways?

Later in the same scene, as the spotlight returns to Peter, we discover another important lesson for us. Jesus had made it clear that he was about to go away and his disciples would not be able to go with him (13:33). Not surprisingly, Peter was concerned and asked Jesus,

> "Lord, where are you going?" Jesus answered, "Where I am going, you cannot follow me now; but you will follow afterward." Peter said to him, "Lord, why can I not follow you now? I will lay down my life for you." (John 13:36–37)

This is now the second time in this upper room scene that Peter has declared his absolute devotion to Jesus (remember the significance of his statement in 13:9). This time, though, we discover that Peter's devotion to

Jesus is not quite up to the level that he thinks it is. Jesus responds to Peter's declaration of absolute commitment this way: "Will you lay down your life for me? Very truly, I tell you, before the cock crows, you will have denied me three times" (13:38). How painful it must have been for Peter to hear those words! How much shame he must have felt for the other disciples to hear Jesus tell him about his impending disloyalty. Jesus' words to Peter, though, are words of warning to every disciple. We often think that we are far more devoted to Jesus than we actually are. And that is a dangerous position in which to be. God's Word says to each of us "not to think of yourself more highly than you ought to think, but to think with sober judgment, each according to the measure of faith that God has assigned" (Rom 12:3). In an age where society trains us to think more highly of ourselves than we should, these words need to be heard and taken to heart by every disciple of Jesus.

In John 18, we once again find Peter returning to center stage. Jesus is with his disciples in the Garden of Gethsemane. As a mob comes to arrest him, Peter takes action. He owns a sword and he knows how to use it! Perhaps Peter was eager to show Jesus that when he said he was willing to lay down his life for him (13:37), he meant it. Jesus' response to Peter, though, teaches us an important lesson. Peter thought he knew the appropriate action to take in those circumstances as a disciple. As one of Jesus' most devoted followers, surely his role was to protect Jesus from those who would harm him. Peter, though, was still thinking in human terms. As readers of the Gospel of John, we have known from the opening words that Jesus is God: "In the beginning was the Word, and the Word was with God, and the Word was God" (1:1). Why would *God* need help from anyone? More important, though, are Jesus' words to Peter: "Am I not to drink the cup that the Father has given me?" (18:11). How often do we fail to grasp God's purposes and thus foolishly act in a way that actually goes against those purposes? Disciples of Jesus are careful to immerse themselves in the Word of God so that they will understand how God works and respond appropriately in the challenging situations of life.

In John 20, we are told that Peter "went into the tomb" and "saw" what was there. The Beloved Disciple, on the other hand, "went in . . . saw and believed" (20:8). This is followed by an explanatory comment that points to an important lesson about discipleship: "for they had not yet understood the Scripture, that it was necessary for him to rise from the dead" (20:9, our translation). The point of this explanatory comment is that prior to that point in time Jesus' disciples had failed to connect what they were seeing in life with the Scriptures. Now, the Beloved Disciple does so. And in doing so, he shows disciples today the importance of learning to allow God's Word to shape their understanding of reality. Jesus' disciples should have grasped far sooner that Jesus had come to die for the sins of the world and to be raised from the dead. He had repeatedly told them so. Even at this point in the story, though, Peter failed to "get it." But the Beloved Disciple at last sees and believes.

In Peter's final interaction with Jesus in John 21, we also learn some important lessons about discipleship. First, we see the heart of a disciple. As seven of Jesus' disciples are in a boat after a night of fishing (21:1–3), when Peter discovers that Jesus is standing on the shore, everything changes for him in that moment. Suddenly, nothing else matters. The normal rules of life no longer apply. He *must* be with Jesus. And he shows no embarrassment about leaving the other disciples to do the work of getting the boat to shore, much like Mary showed no embarrassment about sitting at the feet of Jesus while Martha prepared the meal (Luke 10:38–42). Peter's actions thus illustrate the attitude that Jesus calls every disciple to embrace:

> "Whoever comes to me and does not hate father and mother, wife and children, brothers and sisters, yes, and even life itself, cannot be my disciple." (Luke 14:26)

This is not a call to stop caring for other people or to shirk our responsibilities; it is a call to make sure that our devotion to Jesus is absolute. There is nothing in life that should have a higher priority than following Jesus. Peter illustrates that for us in his urgent swim to shore.

In 21:20–22, we find Jesus making it clearer to Peter what it looks like to be his disciple in practice. Prior to the epilogue, Peter seems to be a person who wants to follow Jesus on his own terms,[13] or at least based on his limited understanding of who Jesus is and what Jesus has come to do. After his restoration (21:15–19), though, Peter appears to come to grips with what it means to be a disciple on Jesus' terms, something the Beloved Disciple had been doing all along. We discover in the book of Acts just how Peter ultimately responded to Jesus' words at the end of the Gospel of John. Not only does Peter lay aside all other pursuits and foolish questions to follow Jesus (21:22), but he also becomes a shepherd to Jesus' sheep. In other

---

13. Resseguie, "Beloved Disciple," 547.

words, Peter finally "becomes the Pastor who loves Jesus and who is loved by Jesus even if he had failed from time to time."[14]

Before we conclude our discussion of the character of Peter in the Gospel of John, we need to recognize that we have only painted a partial picture. Although Peter is often depicted as an unruly pupil who needs to be frequently corrected by his teacher in John 13–21, he tends to be portrayed more favorably earlier in the narrative. After all, it is Peter who beautifully acknowledges Jesus' identity as Messiah in John 6 and chooses to continue as his follower even as many are abandoning Jesus: "Simon Peter answered him, 'Lord, to whom can we go? You have the words of eternal life. We have come to believe and know that you are the Holy One of God'" (6:68–69). This and other earlier events in Peter's life with Jesus remind us that there is more to the character of Peter than we have been able to consider in our brief study. When we read Peter's commendable confession of faith in John 6 along with what we have seen in John 13–21, we are reminded that following Jesus often involves moments of success in our discipleship combined with moments of failure (Peter's denials). In John 6, Peter had not only "seen the light" and come to understand who Jesus was, he had also given Jesus his allegiance. This one-time act of commitment to Jesus, though, did not keep him from later stumbling as he walked along the path of discipleship. The key was that in the end Peter remained a devoted follower of Jesus and had learned from his failures.

Lessons in Discipleship: The Beloved Disciple

When the Beloved Disciple is first introduced in 13:23, he is reclining next to Jesus. The language that is used (Greek: "on the bosom of Jesus") is important. It is the same language that was used earlier in the Gospel of John to characterize Jesus' intimate relationship with the Father: "No one has ever seen God. It is God, the only Son, who is close to the Father's heart [Greek: "on the bosom of the Father"], who has made him known" (1:18). Thus, the Beloved Disciple's relationship with Jesus is implicitly compared to Jesus' relationship to the Father through the use of parallel language. Although we will not explore in any detail the way that God communicates this in the Gospel of John, it is fair to say that one of the primary focuses of John's portrayal of the life and teachings of Jesus is the opportunity that Jesus presents to each of his followers to enjoy the kind of intimacy with him

14. Labahn, "Simon Peter," 167.

Peter and the Beloved Disciple

that the Beloved Disciple enjoyed during Jesus' time on earth.[15] Modern disciples might wish that they could recline at a meal with Jesus and be able to simply lean back and ask him any question. This sort of intimacy with Jesus, though, is precisely what is offered to the new covenant people of God:

> Let us therefore approach the throne of grace with boldness, so that we may receive mercy and find grace to help in time of need. (Heb 4:16)

What Jesus has done for us through his sacrificial death and resurrection has opened the way for us to come to his very throne with *boldness* in our time of need. What a privilege! More than that, the Gospel of John reminds us that as we pursue the path of discipleship, seeking to live a life of obedience to Jesus' commands, the result will be incredible intimacy with the Father, Son, and Holy Spirit (see 14:15-24). What the Beloved Disciple experienced can be the experience of every disciple of Jesus today.

The Beloved Disciple models for us the steady, stable devotion to God that Jesus wants to see in every disciple. While Peter's passion was commendable, it often got him into trouble. He was frequently a loyal but misguided disciple. The Beloved Disciple, on the other hand, showed that his intimacy with Jesus had led to maturity in his discipleship. More than that, it had driven out all fear. When every other disciple abandoned Jesus in his darkest hour as he hung on the cross, the Beloved Disciple was standing by Jesus' side (19:26). And he was not there only for moral support; he was waiting for any last instructions Jesus might have for him. So, when Jesus tells him to care for his mother, the Beloved Disciple obeys without question (19:27).

The Beloved Disciple's steady devotion to Jesus, though, was no less passionate than Peter's devotion. He was the one who ran with all his might to the tomb of Jesus to find out what had happened (20:4). Unlike Peter,

---

15. See Culy, *Echoes*. Jesus, who is in the bosom of the Father, is the revealer of the Father, while the Beloved Disciple, who is in the bosom of Jesus, is the revealer of Jesus. If one wants to know what God the Father is like, he or she should look to Jesus who reveals Him, and if one wants to know what Jesus is like, he or she should look to the Beloved Disciple (the Gospel of John), who reveals Jesus. As Jesus has an intimate relationship with the Father, so the Beloved Disciple has an intimate relationship with Jesus. Just as Jesus is uniquely able to make his Father known, so the Beloved Disciple is uniquely able to make Jesus known. Resseguie notes that "several traits blend together to portray the beloved disciple as the one who has the ideal point of view of the gospel; his intimacy with Jesus; his fidelity; his ability to see what others apparently do not perceive." Resseguie, *Strange Gospel*, 162.

though, his passion for Jesus quickly led to belief (20:8). And that belief was expressed in following Jesus faithfully. Like Peter (21:7), the Beloved Disciple could not help himself; he had to be with Jesus. Even during a private conversation between Jesus and Peter, the Beloved Disciple was quietly trailing behind them so that he could be close to Jesus (21:20). In short, we see in the Beloved Disciple a picture of what the life of one who is very close to Jesus should look like.[16]

Reading in Stereo: Peter and the Beloved Disciple

It is worth noting that in almost every passage where the Beloved Disciple is mentioned in the Gospel of John, he is contrasted with Simon Peter. And this contrast helps highlight some of the most important lessons to be learned from these two major characters. We see nothing but stable devotion to Jesus from the Beloved Disciple. And that quiet stable devotion is accompanied by deep intimacy with Jesus. His devotion is showcased in the fact that the Beloved Disciple is willing to put himself in danger by following Jesus into the high priest's courtyard (18:15). The fact that Peter repeatedly denies his relationship to Jesus in this same scene (18:17, 25, 27) stands in sharp contrast. This scene, then, portrays Peter's temporary lack

---

16. The Beloved Disciple's devotion to Jesus may be alluded to before he is formally introduced into the narrative. At the very beginning of Jesus' ministry, we are told that two of John the Baptist's disciples saw Jesus and followed Him (1:35–40). While Andrew is named as one of the two disciples, scholars tend to believe that the other disciple, who was unnamed, was the Beloved Disciple. See, e.g., Brown, *Gospel According to John*, 73; Resseguie, "Beloved Disciple," 548; Bauckham, *Testimony of the Beloved Disciple*, 84–85. These two disciples are said to "follow" Jesus (1:37, 38) and "remain" with Him (1:39). Later, toward the end of the Gospel, as Peter denies Jesus, the Beloved Disciple remains faithful (18:15–17); as Peter abandons Jesus at the cross, the Beloved Disciple stands by Jesus (19:26–27); and as Peter is commanded to follow Jesus, we find the Beloved Disciple already following Jesus (21:20–22). Thus, the Gospel is "bracketed by the verbal threads 'follow' in 1:37, 38 and 21:20, and 'remain' in 1:38, 39 and 21:22, 23. The *inclusio* reinforces the Beloved Disciple's unique status among the disciples: he has followed and remained with Jesus from beginning to end." Resseguie, "Beloved Disciple," 548. Bennema notes: "It can hardly be a coincidence that the Beloved Disciple's first and last appearances are marked by the *inclusio* of the verbs "follow" and "remain" in 1:37–39 and 21:20, 22." Bennema, *Encountering Jesus*, 301. While we want to be careful not to go beyond what the biblical text actually says, if these scholars are correct, we would find a Beloved Disciple who follows Jesus (in faith and belief) and remains (continues) in a faithful relationship right to the end. Either way, the Beloved Disciple is likely presented as the epitome of a genuine disciple of Jesus in the Gospel of John.

of loyalty to Jesus, while the Beloved Disciple's status as a faithful disciple, even in a very dangerous and stressful situation, remains intact.

The same is true at the crucifixion scene. Of Jesus' twelve disciples, only the Beloved Disciple is present as Jesus dies, along with some faithful, fearless women (19:25–27). Peter is noticeably absent. Three things stand out in this scene as we continue to consider the character pairing of Peter and the Beloved Disciple. First, we see the validity of the old saying, "Actions speak louder than words." Peter had assured Jesus of his absolute devotion, even if it meant dying for him (13:37), only to repeatedly deny his relationship with Jesus in the face of being publicly exposed as Jesus' disciple. Peter *claimed* to be devoted to Jesus; the Beloved Disciple *showed* his devotion to Jesus through his actions. As Jesus hung on the cross, Peter was nowhere to be seen. The Beloved Disciple, on the other hand, presumably put his own life on the line to associate with Jesus during his darkest hour. His quiet devotion to Jesus demonstrated mature discipleship, while Peter's boastful, or at least overstated devotion to Jesus showed that he still needed to grow to maturity in his faith.

Second, it is not insignificant that Jesus entrusts the care of his mother to the Beloved Disciple rather than to Peter. And as he does so, we once again see the actions of the Beloved Disciple demonstrating his devotion to Jesus: "And from that hour the disciple took her into his own home" (19:27). Jesus commands, the Beloved Disciple obeys. He doesn't say, "Jesus, what about your brother James? Shouldn't he be the one to care for your mother?" He simply hears and obeys. This is the mark of every genuine disciple of Jesus.

Notice also the pattern that the Beloved Disciple presents for us. Disciples of Jesus love disciples of Jesus! Those who are devoted to the Messiah will be devoted to caring for the needs of his other followers. Or, in the words of Jesus, they will "love one another." It should not surprise us that it is the Beloved Disciple, the apostle John, who repeats this command of Jesus over and over in his writings (John 13:35; 15:12, 17; 1 John 3:11, 14, 16, 23; 4:7, 11). The Beloved Disciple not only insisted that disciples pay attention to Jesus' command to "love one another," he also modeled that love. And his presence at the cross in contrast to Peter's absence helps drive home this point.

Third, in responding to Jesus' request to care for his mother, the Beloved Disciple also reminds us that Jesus' disciples are eager to follow him and do whatever he asks of them. The Beloved Disciple eagerly embraces the mother of Jesus as his own. He does not think of obeying Jesus as a burden or inconvenience. He views it as a privilege. As one who has been in a deep and intimate relationship with Jesus, he values what Jesus values. He is eager to please the One whom he loves and the One by whom he is loved. In the Beloved Disciple, we find a model disciple who follows Jesus to the cross, is present with Jesus during his time of agony, stands ready to do whatever Jesus asks of him, and is faithful to carry out the commission the Lord gives him. If we want to know what it looks like to be a disciple of Jesus, the Beloved Disciple provides a wonderful model! And that model is fleshed out through contrast with the character of Peter.

The contrast between Peter and the Beloved Disciple continues in the resurrection scene. We are not surprised to find that the Beloved Disciple outruns Peter to the tomb after hearing from Mary that the tomb is empty (20:1–4). Just as the Beloved Disciple was loved *by* Jesus, so also the Beloved Disciple himself loved Jesus and could not wait for Peter to keep up with him; he had to find out what was happening. And his deep devotion to Jesus led him to see and believe what Peter was slow to see and believe. We are given no indication that Peter believed when he saw the empty tomb and Jesus' burial cloths lying there. He simply went into the tomb and saw what was there, while the Beloved Disciple entered, saw, and *believed*. These narrative details do not serve to critique Peter's faith per se. Rather, they highlight the Beloved Disciple's devotion, and in doing so they present us with a pattern of discipleship. We already saw that the Beloved Disciple was quick to respond with obedience to Jesus' commands (19:26–27). Now we see that he is quick to respond to God's revelation of Jesus' resurrection with belief. Disciples are quick to both believe and to act.

In the final chapter of the Gospel of John, as we consider the contrasting actions of the Beloved Disciple and Peter as they realize that it is Jesus calling to them from the shore, we see two positive examples of what it looks like to be a disciple. In this case, their responses to Jesus together serve to provide a robust picture of what discipleship looks like. When the Beloved Disciple hears Jesus' instruction to put the net down on the right side of the boat and sees the result, he once again believes. He combines what he heard with what he saw and he concludes: "It is the Lord!" (21:7). The Beloved Disciple's intimate relationship with Jesus resulted in him quickly recognizing the Lord when Jesus' other disciples did not. *How* he recognized Jesus, though, is important. He did not immediately recognize Jesus' voice, but when he saw the outcome of what the man on the beach had told them to do, knowing the character of Jesus, he quickly concluded that the man on the beach had to be Jesus. This reminds us that recognizing when it is Jesus who is asking us to do something requires that we first *know* Jesus. And knowing Jesus requires that we immerse ourselves in the Word of God to help ensure that the Jesus that we follow is in fact the Jesus of Scripture.

Notice also the contrast between the Beloved Disciple's response (recognition) and Peter's response in this passage. In the previous scene, when the two of them raced to the empty tomb and we learned that the Beloved Disciple outran Peter, we were presented with a disciple whose devotion to Jesus spurred him to run with all his might to be "with Jesus." Here, we see the same intense devotion in Peter. The boat was only about one hundred yards from shore (21:8), but Peter could not wait for the boat to get there. He forgot his role on the boat and plunged into the water in an effort to get to Jesus as fast as he could. He had to be with Jesus! This, too, is the mark of a genuine disciple.

Lessons in Discipleship: Jesus' Interactions with Peter and the Beloved Disciple

Finally, let's consider how Jesus' interactions with Peter and the Beloved Disciple shed further light on what it means to live as Jesus' disciple in this world. When Jesus tells Peter that he would eventually die on a cross, the apostle John supplies us with commentary on Jesus' statement: "He said this to indicate the kind of death by which he would glorify God" (21:19). This shocking statement reminds us that Jesus expects his disciples to "deny themselves and take up their cross daily and follow" him (Luke 9:23), wherever he leads, trusting in his goodness and in God's good purposes for us.

In the final scene with Peter, we find not only Peter's unbridled devotion to Jesus as he dives into the water to swim to shore where Jesus is waiting, but we also find Jesus tenderly guiding Peter's passion in a healthy direction. Peter has learned that he will one day not only be executed, but will, like Jesus, die by crucifixion. When he spots the Beloved Disciple trailing behind, he wonders how his fellow disciple will die. Jesus' words provide a powerful lesson for every disciple: "If it is my will that he remain until I come, what is that to you? Follow me!" (21:22). In other words, as Peter asks what is going to happen to John, Jesus responds, "That is not your concern. That should not be your focus. Your focus should be on following me. Don't worry about what other people are doing. Don't worry about *their* future. Make sure that *your* future is a life dedicated to living for my glory and doing all that I, your Lord, tell you to do."

Many of us tend to focus on other people, rather than focusing on serving the Lord in the ways he wants us to serve him. Many of us focus on insignificant questions in life that only serve to get our attention off of what it should be on, including insignificant theological questions! Jesus tells us, "You follow me!" (21:22, our translation).[17] Following Jesus is ultimately all that matters in this life. In fact, "You follow me!" are the last words of Jesus in the Gospel of John, much like the Great Commission records the last words of Jesus in the Gospel of Matthew. They serve not only as Peter's final lesson in discipleship in John's Gospel, but as our final lesson as well. Those who belong to Jesus, follow him.[18]

Questions for Disciples

1. Think about Jesus' interaction with Peter in the foot washing scene in John 13. Are there areas in your life, where God's will for you is clear, but you think that you know better? What parts of your thinking about God or about what the life of a disciple of Jesus should look like need to be corrected? Are you willing to respond to God with repentance and reaffirmation of your full devotion to Jesus, like Peter did, when you are corrected by God's Word or by a godly brother or sister in Christ?

2. How long has it been since you sat down and carefully considered just how devoted to Christ you really are? Peter had misconceptions about his level of devotion to Jesus. Is the same true of you? What steps do you need to take to help ensure that you do not deny Jesus in the midst of difficult trials in life?

3. In the Garden of Gethsemane, Peter's love for Jesus led him to act in an inappropriate way. Jesus did not need Peter to defend him; he needed Peter to understand God's purpose for him and act accordingly. Are there areas in your life where you might be trying to "serve

---

17. Including "You" better reflects the emphasis in the Greek text.

18. Jesus does not need to issue this same directive to the Beloved Disciple, since he has been faithfully following Jesus from the very beginning. See Bauckham, *Testimony of the Beloved Disciple*, 84.

Peter and the Beloved Disciple

God" with misguided worldly wisdom? How often are you tempted to "help God out," when circumstances aren't going the way you would hope?

4. Recall Peter's actions in John 21 when he discovered that Jesus was on the shore, while he was in the boat. He could not wait another moment to be with Jesus. Does Peter's overwhelming eagerness to be with Jesus reflect your eagerness to be with him? If not, what in your life is robbing you of that eagerness to spend time in Jesus' presence?

5. At the end of John 21, Peter appears to finally come to grips with the need to follow Jesus on Jesus' terms. Have you taken the time to study God's Word so that you understand how God expects a disciple to live? Have you embraced God's way of following Jesus? Or are you still trying to follow him on your own terms?

6. Have you ever felt the shame of failing to be loyal to Jesus like Peter did when he denied him? How does Jesus' compassion in giving Peter the opportunity to reaffirm his devotion to him in John 21:15–17 encourage you to repent and reaffirm your devotion to Jesus when you fail as a disciple? How does this passage remind us that we can still choose to serve God no matter what our past failures have been?

7. At the crucifixion scene, all the disciples, except the Beloved Disciple, fled. When it comes to being publicly identified with Jesus, what circumstances might cause you to be afraid and hide?

10

Thomas

More than a Doubter

IN THIS CHAPTER, WE will explore one other feature of character pairing in the narrative of the Gospel of John. We saw with Mary in chapter 8 that one character can be paired with different characters in different scenes. In John 20–21, we find a similar phenomenon. On the one hand, these chapters invite us to compare and contrast the actions of Peter and the Beloved Disciple, as we have seen. We should also recognize that there is actually a *third* major character in these chapters: Thomas.[1] As we consider the character of Thomas, we will first examine how his character has been developed throughout the Gospel of John. We will then consider how his grouping with the Beloved Disciple and Peter at the end of John's Gospel helps us to understand more fully the nature of discipleship.

Thomas appears seven times in four different episodes within the Gospel of John (11:16; 14:5; 20:24–28; 21:2). He is, of course, best known for his refusal to believe that Jesus had been raised from the dead without physical proof of the resurrection, spawning the common expression, "doubting Thomas." Some recent scholars have actually questioned whether Thomas genuinely doubted Jesus' resurrection at all, suggesting that he simply wanted the same courtesy of physical proof afforded the other disciples on Easter Sunday.[2] Although this assessment is an inadequate analysis of the

---

1. Mary Magdalene actually makes a fourth major character.
2. See Popp, "Thomas," 516; see also Bennema, *Encountering Jesus*, 290, 292.

character of Thomas, in our view, there is clearly more to Thomas in the Gospel of John than is often recognized.³

The first episode where Thomas appears is in the account of the raising of Lazarus in John 11. As we have already seen, when Jesus was told that his dear friend Lazarus was seriously ill (11:3), he did not take immediate action. Instead, after waiting two days, he told his disciples that they would be returning to Judea where Lazarus lived (11:7). His plan to go back to Judea caused great concern among his disciples, since "the Jews" had just tried to kill Jesus there (11:8). But Jesus insisted that it was necessary: "Our friend Lazarus has fallen asleep, but I am going there to awaken him" (11:11). We are not surprised when Jesus' disciples once again misunderstand his comment, thinking that Lazarus was literally asleep and thus would soon recover (11:12). Jesus responded to their confusion by making it clear that Lazarus had, in fact, died (11:14) and he was going to him (11:15). It is at this point in the narrative that Thomas briefly comes into the spotlight. Recognizing the danger that Jesus will be in, Thomas urges the other disciples: "Let us also go, that we may die with him" (11:16).

These are significant words of devotion to Jesus from "doubting Thomas." Jesus will soon tell his disciples, "No one has greater love than this, to lay down one's life for one's friends" (15:13). Modern readers sometimes think that Jesus' words in 15:13 were a new teaching. In reality, though, he was expressing conventional wisdom that was well-known and embraced in the Greco-Roman world and well-known to Thomas and the rest of the disciples. Thomas's words to his fellow disciples in 11:16, then, were the strongest declaration of devotion to Jesus that he could make. And he was urging his fellow disciples to do the same. While Thomas, like Peter, ultimately failed to live up to his expression of devotion to Jesus, he nevertheless revealed here a strong desire to deny himself, take up his cross, and follow him. There is thus more to this character that we know as Thomas than just being a doubter.

The second scene where Thomas appears is found in John 14. Jesus was trying to encourage his disciples by telling them that he was about to go away to prepare a place for them in his Father's house (14:1–4). After telling his disciples that they "know the way" to where he was going (14:4),

---

3. Keener rightly points out that Thomas's skepticism in the absence of a sign "reflects a thread that runs throughout the Gospel: many respond to signs with faith (1:50; 10:38; 11:15, 40; 14:11) and refuse faith without signs (4:48; 6:30), but unless this faith matures into discipleship, it must prove inadequate in the end (8:30–31)." Keener, *Gospel of John*, 2:1208.

Thomas responded, "Lord, we do not know where you are going. How can we know the way?" (14:5). As readers, we do not know whether the plural "we" indicates that all of the disciples shared in Thomas's confusion, with Thomas serving as their spokesman, or whether the "we" indicates that Thomas was hiding his own confusion behind the cover of the entire group.4 What is clear in this scene is that Thomas, like his fellow disciples, did not understand what Jesus was saying.

On the one hand, the narrator likely chooses to record Thomas's role in this scene to exemplify the disciples' propensity for misunderstanding the words of Jesus. On the other hand, his question here, combined with his statement in 11:16, might lead us to conclude that Thomas displayed an eager desire to follow Jesus, whether that meant dying with him (11:16) or entering the Father's presence with him (14:5). What many fail to notice in the narrative flow of the Gospel of John, however, is the fact that in each of these scenes where Thomas is in view, and with many other conversations within the gospel, Jesus appears intentionally to make statements that lead his followers and others to ask for clarification, with their questions in turn setting up some of his more profound revelatory declarations. In other words, though misunderstanding is clearly an important motif in the Gospel of John,5 Jesus frequently precipitates the misunderstanding in order to accomplish his own revelatory and discipleship purposes. In this case, he leads Thomas to ask, "How can we know the way?" (14:5) in order to set up one of his most famous statements in John's Gospel: "I am the way, and the truth, and the life. No one comes to the Father except through me" (14:6). As we think about the character of Thomas, then, we should perhaps be more charitable in assessing his seeming lack of intellectual acumen. Jesus regularly leads him toward a deeper understanding of his identity through speaking in a figurative or opaque manner.

The third and most significant appearance of Thomas is found in the episode following the account of Jesus' resurrection in 20:24–29. Prior to Thomas's personal encounter with the risen Jesus, the Lord had presented himself alive to Mary Magdalene (20:11–18) and then to his inner group of disciples (20:19–23). For some unrecorded reason, Thomas was not with the other disciples when Jesus appeared to them. Just as Mary had previously testified to the disciples about her encounter with the risen Lord (20:18), the other disciples testify to Thomas about their experience with

---

4. See Bennema, *Encountering Jesus*, 289.
5. See Culy, *Echoes*, 104–7.

the risen Jesus (20:25a). Despite this eyewitness account of Jesus' resurrection, however, Thomas dramatically declares his need for tangible proof: "Unless I see the mark of the nails in his hands, and put my finger in the mark of the nails and my hand in his side, I will not believe" (20:25b).[6]

Before considering how the character of Thomas is presented in comparison to the characters of Mary, Peter, and the Beloved Disciple in John 20, we first need to recognize another comparison that is presented in the narrative. We had just encountered a vivid scene where Jesus appeared to all of the remaining disciples, except Thomas (20:19–23), followed by a brief comment on how Thomas had responded when he was told of Jesus' appearance (20:24–25). Although it occurs a week later chronologically, Jesus appears to Thomas in the very next scene in the narrative. And these two scenes are carefully tied together by noting that (1) they take place in the same house (20:26); (2) the doors were shut and locked in both cases (20:19, 26); (3) the disciples were gathered together, with the exception of Thomas on the first occasion (20:19, 26); (4) "Jesus came and stood among them"[7] (20:19, 26); (5) Jesus showed them his hands and his side (20:20, 27); and (6) Jesus said, "Peace be with you" (20:19, 26). By introducing each of the two scenes with virtually the same language, the narrator invites us to compare the two episodes to discover what they communicate when read together. We will focus our attention on the character contrasts in these scenes.[8]

In Jesus' first appearance to his disciples in 20:19–23, the focus was on the commission he was giving them as his ambassadors, the giving of the Holy Spirit, and the authority with which Jesus invested them. In the second appearance (20:26–29), the focus is firmly on Thomas and his faith. Jesus tells him, "Put your finger here and see my hands. Reach out your hand and put it in my side" (20:27). In other words, Jesus responds to Thomas's "doubt" in his resurrection by offering the very evidence Thomas

---

6. Culpepper sees Thomas as a model of a disciple "who understands Jesus' flesh but not his glory," and is thus the opposite of Peter, "who saw Jesus' glory but could not accept his suffering." Culpepper, *Anatomy*, 123.

7. There is slight variation in the Greek here.

8. There are a number of other important contrasts as well. During his first appearance to his disciples, Jesus does three things that are not repeated when Thomas is present: He commissions the disciples (20:21); he gifts them with the Holy Spirit (20:22); and he invests them with authority (20:23). On the question of how Jesus' post-resurrection gifting of the Spirit in this passage, which has been called a "Johannine Pentecost," compares with the coming of the Holy Spirit in Acts 2, see Burge's helpful discussion of the various theories. Burge, *John*, 558–61.

demanded.⁹ Jesus then issues an apparent rebuke to Thomas: "Do not doubt but believe" (20:28c). How does Thomas respond? He responds with one the greatest confessions of faith found in all of Scripture: "My Lord and my God!" (20:28). Thomas not only submits himself to the lordship of Jesus, but also acknowledges Jesus as God, echoing the opening words of the Gospel of John: "the Word was with God, and the Word was God" (1:1). The Gospel of John thus effectively ends as it began, with a clear and dramatic revelation that Jesus is God.¹⁰

After Thomas's climactic confession, Jesus offers the only beatitude found in the Gospel of John: "Have you believed because you have seen me? Blessed are those who have not seen and yet have come to believe" (20:29). Interestingly, Jesus does not congratulate Thomas on his advancement away from unbelief to belief, nor does he formally confer on him the same commission, gift of the Holy Spirit, and authority that he had conferred on the other disciples a week earlier when Thomas was absent.¹¹ Instead, Jesus offers an exhortation to Thomas to choose to believe¹² and then pronounces a blessing upon those who, unlike Thomas, would choose belief without actually seeing and experiencing Jesus in the flesh (20:25).

Lessons in Discipleship: Thomas in John 20

When modern disciples of Jesus think about model disciples in the New Testament, Thomas does not tend to make the list. After all, who wants to be a Doubting Thomas? As we have seen, though, there is far more to Thomas than a doubting disciple. In fact, even in John 20, Thomas showcases some critical lessons of discipleship.

First, we find a character grouping in John 20 that helps us to identify a key lesson. In 20:8, the Beloved Disciple chooses to believe that Jesus has risen from the dead when he sees the empty tomb. He has not yet encountered the risen Christ himself. Mary Magdalene, on the other hand,

---

9. The text is silent on whether Thomas followed through with touching Jesus' hands or putting his hand in Jesus' side, since the sight of Jesus before him may have been proof enough to elicit his faith response.

10. For more on the *inclusio* between Thomas's confession and the prologue about the divine nature of Jesus, see Keener, *Gospel of John*, 1211.

11. The fact that Thomas would have received the same commission at some point is suggested by the traditional view that he later brought the gospel to Syria and India; see the *Acts of Thomas*, 11:31, 39.

12. Contra Popp, "Thomas," 522.

believes when she encounters the risen Christ (20:16). The narrative does not present her faith as deficient in any way; it merely presents a different path to faith for her and the Beloved Disciple. And in doing so it reminds us that not all disciples come to faith in the same way. This becomes important background for understanding the path to faith that Thomas takes. Because of his rash statement in 20:25 ("Unless I see the mark of the nails in his hands, and put my finger in the mark of the nails and my hand in his side, I will not believe."), Thomas has often been reduced to an example of what faith does *not* look like. And in a certain sense that is true; but there is more to the story as we will see in a moment. By grouping Thomas with the Beloved Disciple and Mary Magdalene in this passage, the narrative drives us to take a closer look at Thomas's faith.

Second, it is critical that we recognize that Thomas's unbelief quickly gives way to belief when he is confronted by Jesus (see 20:27–28). He does not appear to carry through on his rash declaration: "Unless I see the mark of the nails in his hands, and put my finger in the mark of the nails and my hand in his side, I will not believe" (20:25). This likely helps us to see that Thomas was not so much a doubter as a grief-stricken follower of Jesus who was so overwhelmed by his circumstance that he made a foolish statement. And this reminds us that in the midst of the intense trials of life it is easy to let unbelief creep in, rather than forcing our minds and hearts back to sure promises of God found in Scripture. Jesus had *told* Thomas that he would rise from the dead, but Thomas let his emotions drive his actions, rather than bringing his emotions under the authority of what Jesus had told him.

Third, Thomas's ultimate declaration of faith is not only exemplary, it also serves as an important reminder of all that comes before in the Gospel of John about what it means to be a disciple of Jesus. John's Gospel is a call to believe in Jesus, but not in just *any* Jesus. It is a call to believe in a Jesus who is both Lord and God. To fail to bow before Jesus as Lord—surrendering all that we are to his authority and his purposes for our life—is to fail to have the kind of belief required to be a genuine disciple of Jesus. The Gospel of John, however, also emphasizes the non-negotiable affirmation that Jesus is God. Any belief that comes up short of embracing Jesus' divinity is not a belief that can save someone. True disciples embrace Jesus as Lord and God and there are dramatic, practical implications for both of these critical truths about Jesus' identity.

The Making of a Disciple

Lessons in Discipleship: Jesus with Thomas in John 20

As in the other passages we have considered, we also find important lessons on discipleship flowing out of Jesus' interaction with Thomas in this passage. Many readers are so accustomed to reading this chapter of the Gospel of John through the lens of tradition, which treats Thomas as "Doubting Thomas," that they overlook the language that is used. Jesus' exhortation to Thomas at the end of 20:27 is translated, "Do not doubt but believe" in the NRSV. In the Greek text, though, Jesus does not use a typical word for "doubt."[13] In fact, Jesus is likely not dealing with the concept of doubt here, but rather with the concept of *unbelief*. In other words, he urges him, as the Gospel of John urges readers from beginning to end, to choose to believe Jesus. Better translations of 20:27, then, include, "Do not be faithless, but believe" (CSB; cf. KJV); "Do not disbelieve, but believe" (ESV); and "Do not continue in your unbelief, but believe" (NET).

The overarching agenda of the Gospel of John, and the overarching agenda of Jesus in the Gospel of John, is to invite readers to choose to believe and embrace the identity, mission, teachings, and commands of Jesus. Both Jesus' words and actions in this part of the narrative suggest that the call to discipleship is less about having all of our doubts removed by tangible proof and more about choosing to believe all that God has revealed about Jesus and his call on our life through his Word. It is a call to cease being selective in what we choose to believe from Scripture (which is, by definition, unbelief) and to come to grips with the fact that it is an all or nothing proposition. If God says something in his Word, I do not have a choice as a disciple of Jesus whether or not I will accept it and act on it.

We also should not miss the profound picture of Jesus, the Good Shepherd (10:11), in this passage. Thomas had refused to believe the testimony of the other disciples even though it precisely matched what Jesus had earlier revealed to all of them about his impending death and resurrection. Jesus could have been angry with Thomas. Jesus could have rejected Thomas as a disciple. Jesus could have simply rebuked Thomas for his refusal to believe the testimony of the other disciples. Instead, he graciously offered Thomas the evidence for which Thomas had asked. Along with the exhortation to stop being faithless and believe (20:27), he gently and graciously presented his scarred body to Thomas to bolster his faith. Jesus knows our

---

13. Had the focus been on doubt, we likely would have found the verb διακρίνομαι (*diakrinomai*) here or another term for doubting.

weaknesses. Jesus knows our tendency to slip into unbelief. And he bears with us in our failings, taking steps to build our faith through exposure to both his Word and to his presence and power in the challenges of this life.

Questions for Disciples

1. How does your commitment to follow Jesus wherever he goes compare with Thomas's commitment expressed in 11:16? Are you prepared to follow Jesus when great sacrifice might be required?
2. How does the fact that Jesus is both Lord and God impact your everyday life?
3. Thomas failed to believe Jesus' resurrection even though Jesus had clearly and repeatedly told him that he would die and rise from the dead. Have you ever been so overwhelmed by a severe trial in life that you failed to believe what God has clearly revealed to be true?
4. If Jesus confronted you today, as he did Thomas, what types of unbelief would he urge you to abandon?
5. Are there teachings or commands of Jesus that you have failed to embrace? Have you been selective in believing certain parts of God's Word and ignored or rejected others?
6. How does Jesus' gracious and compassionate response to Thomas's struggle to believe encourage you to take your questions and struggles to Jesus?

11

The Gospel of John and Future Disciples

MOST MODERN BIBLE READERS today are very familiar with these words: "All scripture is inspired by God and is useful for teaching, for reproof, for correction, and for training in righteousness, so that everyone who belongs to God may be proficient, equipped for every good work" (2 Tim 3:16–17). This passage is perhaps most often quoted to remind us of the source of Scripture and its authority. Notice, though, that 2 Tim 3:16–17 focuses more attention on the purpose of Scripture than on its source. And the purpose it sets forth should lead Bible readers to ask a simple question of every passage of Scripture that they read: How exactly does this passage teach me, reprove me, correct me, and train me in righteousness? Or, put another way, how does this passage move me toward maturity as a disciple of Jesus? What we have attempted to show in the preceding chapters is that the goals 2 Tim 3:16–17 set forth for Scripture are accomplished in biblical narratives, in part, as readers give careful attention to the major characters, their actions, and the consequences of those actions. As we do so, we discover important lessons about what it means to live as a devoted follower of the one true God. We have also seen that, at times, the message conveyed through the major characters in narratives will be reinforced or expanded through the use of character pairs or character groups.

Our main purpose for examining the major characters in the Gospel of John, then, has been to demonstrate how studying the narrative in this way can help us understand more fully the characteristics of a genuine disciple of Jesus. As we have encountered various characters in the Gospel of John, we have been implicitly invited to either emulate or avoid those characters' responses to Jesus and his teachings. This, in fact, has always been the way God has communicated through biblical narrative. We are explicitly told, more than once, for example, that the accounts of Israel's history were recorded so that future disciples would have numerous examples of what it looks like to live as the people of God.

> Now these things occurred as examples for us, so that we might not desire evil as they did. (1 Cor 10:6)

> These things happened to them to serve as an example, and they were written down to instruct us, on whom the ends of the ages have come. (1 Cor 10:11)

Biblical narratives thus ultimately remind us that God has not only *told* his people how he wants them to live (e.g., in Leviticus, Deuteronomy, and the New Testament Epistles), but he has also *shown* them how he wants them to live (e.g., through narrative accounts like Genesis, 2 Samuel, the Gospels, and Acts).

This does not mean, of course, that the Gospel of John and other biblical narratives are simply handbooks on how to live a moral life. As John's Gospel itself makes clear, its purpose is to show people how to *have* life (20:31)! Having life, though, goes far beyond receiving the gift of eternal life. It also involves enjoying an abundant life now (10:10) that is characterized by fullness of joy (15:11; 16:24). And those blessings are only realized as disciples of Jesus choose to continue or "abide" in his word (8:31–32). The accounts of the characters Jesus encounters in the Gospel of John, then, are intended as far more than history. They are included to reinforce Jesus' teachings and remind readers that both eternal life and abundant life depend on how one responds to Jesus and his teachings not simply at a point in time (conversion) but throughout their lives as his disciples as they encounter more and more of the truths God has revealed in Scripture.

Like the characters in the Gospel of John, readers today are urged to embrace the truths that Jesus reveals. And like the characters in the Gospel of John, some will struggle to do that. Not every person who ultimately chooses to believe in Jesus will walk the same path toward belief or even walk the same path after they embrace Jesus as the Messiah. Some will quickly believe and go on to show steady devotion to Jesus from beginning to end, like the Beloved Disciple.[1] Others, like most characters in the Gos-

---

1. We do find, however, that the frequent misunderstanding of the twelve disciples is at times apparently attributed to John as well, since he was one of the Twelve (e.g., 12:16; 20:9).

pel of John, will struggle in varying degrees to come to a point of belief in the Messiah. Although the Samaritan woman reaches that point relatively quickly, for example, Nicodemus's struggle to believe seems to span much of John's Gospel.

Choosing to believe in Jesus, however, is not itself the end of the story in the Gospel of John, just as it is not the end of the story in the Christian life. We discover that even those who recognize and embrace Jesus as the Messiah may later falter in their faith. Peter, for example, confesses Jesus to be the Messiah in 6:68–69, only later to deny even knowing him (18:15–18, 25–27). In between these contradictory events, we see Peter failing to understand Jesus' actions (13:6–9) and acting in a rash and misguided manner (18:10). In other words, we see Peter struggling along the path toward mature discipleship. We are encouraged, though, as we see the "end" of Peter's story, at least in the Gospel of John. Despite his spiritual failure in denying Jesus three times, he ultimately reaffirms his devotion to Jesus (21:15–17) and goes on to be used by God to shepherd his people and to help establish the early church (see the book of Acts).[2]

The somewhat convoluted path that Peter walks reminds modern disciples that not everyone will have a smooth and consistent path of discipleship. And the range of responses that we see to Jesus from various characters throughout the Gospel of John, coupled with their diverse backgrounds and circumstances, reminds us that different people face different kinds of obstacles that must be overcome before they are prepared to believe in Jesus and become his disciple. John's Gospel invites modern readers to learn from both those who are quick to believe in Jesus and from those who struggle to understand Jesus' message and identity. And the frank accounts of both the successes and failures of characters like Peter remind modern readers that being a disciple of Jesus is not simply about a one-time choice to believe. Discipleship requires growth. Discipleship requires encountering more of Jesus' teachings and choosing to continue living in light of them, refusing to be selective in which parts of God's Word we will embrace (8:31).

---

2. Other examples of appropriate and inappropriate responses coming from the same character include Philip, who acknowledges Jesus' identity in 1:44–45, but shows ignorance of Jesus' power in 6:5–7 and relationship to the Father in 14:8. Similarly, Andrew confesses Jesus as the Messiah in 1:41, but later also fails to recognize Jesus' power in 6:8–9.

The Gospel of John and Future Disciples

A Final Character Pair

If we had any lingering questions about whether the Gospel of John describes major characters' interactions with Jesus for our instruction today, we need only look at a final character pair that John implicitly presents to readers at the end of the main body of his narrative. In 20:29, future disciples are essentially presented as a character pair with Thomas: "Thomas answered him, 'My Lord and my God!' Jesus said to him, 'Have you believed because you have seen me? *Blessed are those who have not seen and yet have come to believe*'" (John 20:28–29). Here, we are vividly reminded that the Gospel of John was not written as a history book, though it is an account of actual historical events. Nor was it simply intended to impact the lives of the first disciples who read it. Instead, it was written in order to produce *future* disciples, as people over the centuries read it and choose to believe. In 20:29, the words of Jesus, which the apostle John alone records, strikingly set such future disciples as a character group in contrast with the character of Thomas. While Thomas had the privilege of seeing the risen Jesus in the flesh, and having that tangible experience of Jesus fuel his faith, subsequent generations would have to choose to believe without experiencing Jesus in this way, without seeing Jesus' physical form. They would have to rely on the eyewitness testimony of those who observed Jesus' life, teachings, miracles, death, and resurrection, and went on to record their testimony in the New Testament. John's testimony about God becoming flesh and living among us (1:14) presents future disciples with the opportunity for great blessing, blessing that is expressed in the final words of the main body of John's narrative: "But these are written so that *you* may come to believe that Jesus is the Messiah, the Son of God, and that through believing *you* may have life in his name" (20:31).

We should not be surprised by this focus on future disciples at the end of the Gospel of John. After all, from beginning to end, John's Gospel repeatedly holds out the opportunity to *all* to receive eternal life by choosing to believe the testimony that it presents about Jesus.[3] Indeed, the broad exhortation to believe in Jesus that is woven throughout the narrative is driven home through the long list of characters who respond to Jesus with faith and find life through him. We are shown through some characters that belief in Jesus does not require actually seeing him, as Jesus' beatitude

---

3. See, e.g., 1:12; 3:16–18, 36; 5:24; 6:29; 12:44–46. The theme of believing in Jesus is central to the Gospel of John. It is evidenced, in part, through using verb forms associated with "believing" about 100 times. Hillmer, "They Believed in Him," 84.

in 20:29 suggests. Some of the Samaritans believed based on the testimony of the woman who encountered Jesus at the well before they saw and listened to Jesus himself (4:39). The royal official's entire household believed because of his testimony, without ever apparently seeing Jesus themselves (4:50). So, the narrative of the Gospel of John supports and illustrates the truth of Jesus' words in 20:29 that there will be future disciples who believe without seeing him. In fact, Jesus prayed for these future disciples (you and me) in his high priestly prayer (17:20–21). In a very real sense, then, the Gospel of John is *directed* at future disciples and provides extensive guidance not only for how to become Jesus' disciple, but also for how to grow and thrive as his disciples.

As we consider the character pairing of Thomas and future disciples, it is important to note another way that Jesus' words in 20:29 provide a capstone to a key theme in the Gospel of John. John's Gospel places significant emphasis on Jesus' numerous signs, which served to reveal his glory to his followers (2:11). It also, though, makes it clear that faith based merely on such signs, without embracing Jesus' mission, identity, and teachings, is defective faith.[4] By pairing future potential disciples with Thomas in the final scene of his narrative proper, the apostle John encourages modern readers to recognize that their choice to believe is not dependent on seeing Jesus for themselves. To receive the gift of eternal life through Jesus one must act in faith. Indeed, through Jesus' interactions with a range of characters, through his teachings, and through the narrator's commentary, readers are called to abandon any insistence on signs or miracles to prove God's existence or goodness or power and instead choose to take God at his word and act on what he says to be true.[5]

Finally, the Gospel of John puts particular emphasis on one aspect of discipleship, in part by ending on the same thematic note with which it began. We saw the strong emphasis on disciples of Jesus pointing others to him in 1:19–51. This same theme is reiterated in John 20 as Mary Magdalene sees the empty tomb and immediately goes and tells Peter and the Beloved Disciple (20:2). Mary is then given a commission by Jesus to take the message of his resurrection to the other disciples and she does so (20:17–18). After seeing the risen Jesus, the other disciples are quick to tell

---

4. See, e.g., 2:23–25.

5. The character of Thomas certainly reminds us that this can be difficult. And Jesus' response to Thomas reminds us that God sometimes graciously grants us tangible signs to encourage our faith.

The Gospel of John and Future Disciples

Thomas (20:25). Jesus then tells Thomas that there will be people who will believe without seeing, implying that his disciples will tell others about him (20:29). And finally, we see that the Gospel of John itself serves as the apostle John's written testimony about the person and work of Jesus, testimony that is intended to lead others to believe and receive life (20:30–31). The narrative proper[6] thus begins and ends with the same focus, leaving readers with a central calling of discipleship ringing in their ears: A disciple, by definition, tells others what Jesus came to do for them.

In the end, the Gospel of John is not simply about the life and ministry of Jesus; it is about the making of a disciple of Jesus. It points readers today not only to how to become a disciple and receive eternal life, but also how to live as a disciple who possesses eternal life. It makes it clear that no one can truly possess eternal life without embracing the path of discipleship (8:31–32). A simple confession of faith is not enough; every disciple is called to a life of devotion to Jesus. As Dietrich Bonhoeffer has reminded us, "Christianity without discipleship is always Christianity without Christ."[7] Those who claim to be Jesus' followers today must examine themselves to see if they are "living in the faith" (2 Cor 13:5), asking themselves whether they have truly embraced the Jesus of the Bible and chosen to live by ("continue in") his teachings even when they go against conventional wisdom or are uncomfortable for other reasons. As we have seen, particularly with the man born blind (John 9), there is a cost to following Jesus. The world today is no less hostile toward Jesus' followers than the Jewish authorities were in the first century. Those who profess to follow Jesus, but attempt to stay in the shadows as Nicodemus did (John 3), deceive themselves. Those who think they can embrace Jesus and avoid a backlash from their community (9:20–23), deceive themselves. But those who embrace Jesus on his terms will experience an ever-deeper relationship with him. John's Gospel thus not only invites readers to become true disciples of Jesus Christ, showing us clearly how a disciple is made, but also presents for us the glorious blessing that every genuine disciple of Jesus can expect in this life: an abundant life of intimacy with God and fullness of joy regardless of our circumstances!

---

6. Minus the Prologue in 1:1–18 and the Epilogue in John 21.
7. Bonhoeffer, *Cost of Discipleship*, 59.

Questions for Disciples

1. What key lessons stand out that you learned from the characters in the Gospel of John about how to have eternal life and experience the joys of an abundant life?
2. Which character or characters in the Gospel of John do you identify with the most? How might seeing yourself in certain characters help you to grow as a disciple of Jesus?
3. Does your life show that being a witness of Jesus is your central calling as his disciple? What lessons from the Gospel of John might God want you to use to point others to Jesus?
4. As you think about other characters in the Bible, which ones might God want to use to teach you new lessons about discipleship?
5. How should recognizing the different ways that people come to faith or grow in their faith encourage you not to lose heart in your own discipleship journey or when you are sharing your faith with others?

Bibliography

Alter, Robert. *The Art of Biblical Narrative*. New York: Basic, 1981.
Ball, David Mark. *'I Am' in John's Gospel: Literary Function, Background and Theological Implications*. Journal for the Study of the New Testament Supplement Series 124. Sheffield: Sheffield Academic, 1996.
Bauckham, Richard. *The Testimony of the Beloved Disciple: Narrative, History, and Theology in the Gospel of John*. Grand Rapids: Baker Academic, 2007.
Beasley-Murray, John. *John*. Word Biblical Commentary. Waco: Word, 1987.
Beck, David R. "'Whom Jesus Loved': Anonymity and Identity, Belief and Witness in the Fourth Gospel." In *Characters and Characterization in the Gospel of John*, edited by Christopher W. Skinner, 221–39. New York: Bloomsbury T. & T. Clark, 2013.
Bennema, Cornelis. "A Comprehensive Approach to Understanding Character in the Gospel of John." In *Characters and Characterization in the Gospel of John*, edited by Christopher W. Skinner, 36–58. New York: Bloomsbury T. & T. Clark, 2013.
———. *Encountering Jesus: Character Studies in the Gospel of John*. 2nd ed. Minneapolis: Fortress, 2014.
———. "A Theory of Character in the Fourth Gospel with Reference to Ancient and Modern Literature." *Biblical Interpretation* 17 (2009) 375–421.
Berlin, Adele. *Poetics and Interpretation of Biblical Narrative*. Sheffield: Almond, 1983.
Bonhoeffer, Dietrich. *The Cost of Discipleship*. Translated by R. H. Fuller. New York: Touchstone, 1995.
Brown, Raymond E. *The Gospel According to John*. 2 vols. Anchor Bible 29, 29A. Garden City, NY: Doubleday, 1966, 1970.
Burge, Gary M. *John*. NIV Application Commentary. Grand Rapids: Zondervan, 2000.
Byrne, Brendan. "The Faith of the Beloved Disciple and the Community in John 20." *Journal for the Study of the New Testament* 23 (1985) 83–97.
Carson, D. A. *The Gospel According to John*. Grand Rapids: Eerdmans, 1991.
Chennattu, Rekha M. *Johannine Discipleship as a Covenant Relationship*. Peabody, MA: Hendrickson, 2006.
Collins, Raymond. "From John to the Beloved Disciple: An Essay on Johannine Characters." *Interpretation* 49 (1995) 359–69.
———. "Representative Figures." In *These Things Have Been Written: Studies on the Fourth Gospel*, edited by R. F. Collins, 1–45. Louvain Theological & Pastoral Monographs 2. Louvain: Peeters, 1990.

Bibliography

———. "'Who Are You?' Comparison/Contrast and Fourth Gospel Characterization." In *Characters and Characterization in the Gospel of John*, edited by Christopher W. Skinner, 79–95. New York: Bloomsbury T. & T. Clark, 2013.

Coloe, Mary L. "The Woman of Samaria: Her Characterization, Narrative, and Theological Significance." In *Characters and Characterization in the Gospel of John*, edited by Christopher W. Skinner, 182–96. New York: Bloomsbury T. & T. Clark, 2013.

Culpepper, Alan. *Anatomy of the Fourth Gospel*. Philadelphia: Fortress, 1983.

———. "Nicodemus: The Travail of New Birth." In *Character Studies in the Fourth Gospel: Narrative Approaches to Seventy Figures in John*, edited by Steven A. Hunt et al., 249–59. Grand Rapids: Eerdmans, 2013.

Culy, Martin M. *Echoes of Friendship in the Gospel of John*. New Testament Monographs 30. Sheffield: Sheffield Phoenix, 2010.

de Boer, Martinus C. "Andrew: The First Link in the Chain." In *Character Studies in the Fourth Gospel*, edited by Steven A. Hunt et al., 137–50. Grand Rapids: Eerdmans, 2013.

Duvall, J. Scott, and J. Daniel Hays. *Grasping God's Word*. Grand Rapids: Zondervan, 2001.

Hillmer, Melvyn R. "They Believed in Him: Discipleship in the Johannine Tradition." In *Patterns of Discipleship in the New Testament*, edited by Richard N. Longenecker, 77–97. Grand Rapids: Eerdmans, 1996.

Hunt, Steven A., et al., eds. *Character Studies in the Fourth Gospel: Narrative Approaches to Seventy Figures in John*. Grand Rapids: Eerdmans, 2013.

Keener, Craig S. *The Gospel of John*. 2 vols. Peabody, MA: Hendrickson, 2003.

Klink, Edward W. III. "Come and See: Discipleship in John's Gospel." In *Following Jesus Christ: The New Testament Message of Discipleship for Today*, edited by John K. Goodrich and Mark L. Strauss, 60–75. Grand Rapids: Kregel Academic, 2019.

Koester, Craig. *Symbolism in the Fourth Gospel: Meaning, Mystery, Community*. 2nd ed. Minneapolis: Fortress, 2003.

Köstenberger, Andreas J. *John*. Baker Exegetical Commentary of the New Testament. Grand Rapids: Baker Academic, 2004.

———. *Theology of John's Gospel and Letters*. Grand Rapids: Zondervan, 2019.

Labahn, Michael. "Simon Peter: An Ambiguous Character and His Narrative Career." In *Character Studies in the Fourth Gospel: Narrative Approaches to Seventy Figures in John*, edited by Steven A. Hunt et al., 151–67. Grand Rapids: Eerdmans, 2013.

Marguerat, Daniel, and Yvan Bourquin. *How to Read Bible Stories*. Translated by John Bowden. London: SCM, 1999.

Metzger, Bruce M. *A Textual Commentary on the New Testament*. 2nd ed. New York: United Bible Societies, 1994.

Michaels, J. Ramsey. *The Gospel of John*. New International Commentary on the New Testament. Grand Rapids: Eerdmans, 2010.

———. "The Invalid at the Pool: The Man Who Merely Got Well." In *Character Studies in the Fourth Gospel: Narrative Approaches to Seventy Figures in John*, edited by Steven A. Hunt et al., 337–46. Grand Rapids: Eerdmans, 2013.

Moore, Stephen D. *Literary Criticism and the Gospels: The Theoretical Challenge*. New Haven, CT: Yale University Press, 1989.

O'Day, Gail R. "The Gospel of John: Introduction, Commentary, and Reflections." *The New Interpreter's Bible, Volume 9*. Nashville: Abingdon, 1998.

Painter, John. *Reading John's Gospel Today*. Atlanta: John Knox, 1975.

Pate, C. Marvin. *The Writings of John*. Grand Rapids: Zondervan, 2011.

Bibliography

Popp, Thomas. "Thomas: Question Marks and Exclamation Marks." In *Character Studies in the Fourth Gospel*, edited by Steven A. Hunt et al., 504–29. Grand Rapids: Eerdmans, 2013.

Reimer, Andy M. "The Man Born Blind: True Disciple of Jesus." In *Character Studies in the Fourth Gospel: Narrative Approaches to Seventy Figures in John*, edited by Steven A. Hunt et al., 428–38. Grand Rapids: Eerdmans, 2013.

Resseguie, James L. "The Beloved Disciple: The Ideal Point of View." In *Character Studies in the Fourth Gospel: Narrative Approaches to Seventy Figures in John*, edited by Steven A. Hunt et al., 537–49. Grand Rapids: Eerdmans, 2013.

———. *The Strange Gospel: Narrative Design and Point of View in John*. Leiden: Brill, 2001.

Schürer, Emil. *The History of the Jewish People in the Age of Jesus*. Revised and edited by G. Vermes, F. Millar, and M. Black. 4 vols. Edinburgh: T. & T. Clark, 1973–1979.

Skinner, Christopher W., ed. *Characters and Characterization in the Gospel of John*. New York: Bloomsbury T. & T. Clark, 2013.

Strauss, Mark L. *Four Portraits, One Jesus. An Introduction to Jesus and the Gospels*. Grand Rapids: Zondervan, 2007.

Watson, Edward W., and Angela L. Watson. "The Love of God: An Interdisciplinary Approach to Developing and Measuring Spiritual Maturity Based on a Johannine Love Ethic." In *But These are Written: Essays on Johannine Literature in Honor of Professor Benny C. Aker*, edited by Craig S. Keener et al., 153–70. Eugene, OR: Pickwick, 2014.

Wilkins, Michael J. *Following the Master: A Biblical Theology of Discipleship*. Grand Rapids: Zondervan, 1992.

Witherington, Ben III. *What Have They Done to Jesus? Beyond Strange Theories and Bad History—Why We Can Trust the Bible*. New York: HarperOne, 2006.

Author Index

Alter, Robert, ix, x

Ball, David Mark, 43
Bauckham, Richard, 95, 106, 110
Beasley-Murray, John, 41, 78, 98
Beck, David R., 96
Bennema, Cornelis, ix, x, 6, 13, 22, 41, 44, 73, 78, 83, 95, 100, 106, 112, 114
Berlin, Adele, ix, x, 5
Boer, Martinus C. de, 22
Bonhoeffer, Dietrich, 125
Bourquin, Yvan, ix, x
Brown, Raymond E., 73, 98, 106
Burge, Gary M., 31, 41, 100, 115
Byrne, Brendan, 99

Carson, D. A., 78, 91
Chennattu, Rekha M., 2
Collins, Raymond, 5, 86, 95
Coloe, Mary L., 44
Culpepper, Alan, ix, x, 5, 6, 14, 15, 36, 66, 76, 86, 94, 95, 115
Culy, Martin M., ix, 15, 43, 105, 114

Duvall, J. Scott, 12

Hays, J. Daniel, 12
Hillmer, Melvyn R., 3, 13, 35, 123
Hunt, Steven A., ix, x

Keener, Craig S., 35, 40, 41, 44, 56, 77, 85, 94, 95, 113, 116
Klink, Edward W. III, 3
Koester, Craig, 56
Köstenberger, Andreas J., 76, 77

Labahn, Michael, 100, 104

Marguerat, Daniel, ix, x
Metzger, Bruce M., 61
Michaels, J. Ramsey, 65, 66, 75
Moore, Stephen D., 7

O'Day, Gail R., 40

Painter, John., 14
Pate, C. Marvin, 75
Popp, Thomas, 112, 116
Reimer, Andy M., 73, 75, 78
Resseguie, James L., 97, 98, 103, 105, 106

Schürer, Emil, 72, 73
Skinner, Christopher W., ix, x
Strauss, Mark L., 45

Watson, Angela L., ix
Watson, Edward W., ix
Wilkins, Michael J., 7
Witherington, Ben III, 94

www.ingramcontent.com/pod-product-compliance
Lightning Source LLC
Chambersburg PA
CBHW020855160426
43192CB00007B/928